Essential Concepts of Cross-Cultural Management

Essential Concepts of Cross-Cultural Management: Building On What We All Share

Lawrence A. Beer

Essential Concepts of Cross-Cultural Management: Building On What We All Share

First published in 2012 by
Business Expert Press, LLC
222 East 46th Street, New York, NY 10017
www.businessexpertpress.com

ISBN-13: 978-1-60649-389-2 (paperback)

ISBN-13: 978-1-60649-390-8 (e-book)

DOI 10.4128/ 9781606493908

A publication in the Business Expert Press International Business collection

Collection ISSN: 1948-2752 (print)
Collection ISSN: 1948-2760 (electronic)

Cover design by Jonathan Pennell
Interior design by Exeter Premedia Services Private Ltd., Chennai, India

First edition: 2012

10 9 8 7 6 5 4 3 2 1

Printed in the United States of America.

Abstract

The purpose and/or promotional promise of almost all textbooks concerning the global environment of commerce is to help the reader understand and appreciate the economic, political, and technological context in which international business operates. This defined approach is tantamount to placing three wheels on a car and expecting it to drive smoothly. It cannot be operated without the balance that a fourth one provides, and that required wheel is culture. In the modern era of globalization, managers venturing forth to engage alien societies must be armed with cross-cultural skill sets lest they travel on feet of clay. Most academic texts and encased individual chapters targeting business students are awash with a confusing maze of intersecting theoretical-based value determinants to define and characterize cultural differences. On the other side of the culture subject are multitudes of guidebooks for executives led by the popular series *Kiss, Bow or Shake Hands* highlighting disparities as one does business in countless singular societies around the world. Both approaches center on memorizing collections of applied principles and/or factual orientations. A more concise, simple, and practical approach is required that cuts through the complicated cultural matrix.

The book is divided into three sections. The first explains to the novice, while reminding those acquainted with the subject, how culture acts as the prime driver of our life—the filter of our senses and the guide of our values, hence the measurement barometer upon which all our decisions and behavior are constructed. The use of culture in a commercial setting is introduced with research generated guidelines to complete the introduction for managers. The next section examines how cross-cultural determinants should function as a worthwhile tool in cross-cultural engagement proposing a two-step concentration. First, if we are different, what is the degree of separation, a step to getting people to recognize that diverse societies are not necessarily polar opposites, black and white programmed absolutes, as there exists a gray space of shared common ground. The duality factor, all cross-cultural determinants contain dual elements, mirror opposites of each other inherent in all cultural dimensions allows one to take notice of similarities as opposed to focusing attention on differences, that understanding and appreciating that the minor side, a dormant or hidden dimension in one culture can be matched up with the dominant side of another's culture thereby allowing mutual cooperation pathways to be constructed. Second, that cultures can be defined as operating on four basic parameters or value determinants and that they can be further reduced to a central or core controlling one—individualism versus collectivism. The final section offers the practical application of these aforementioned techniques to navigate the cross-cultural milieu and become a cultural detective. Concluding comments are then offered on collateral issues to strengthen the skill sets of managers across the cultural divide.

Keywords

International business, globalization, cultural anthropology, cultural determinants, cultural dimensions, international trade, cultural diversity, cultural encounters

Contents

Preface

The preface allows an author to express the inspiration(s) for the book while adding personal thoughts on the subject matter. The stimulus for writing on culture began in the mid-1960s during my undergraduate education in the School of Management at Boston University where I majored in International Business. Not one course, much less one chapter in any of my textbooks, offered a cross-cultural introduction to the global business world. No instructor gave a lecture or even commented on the matter. Later in my managerial career, and upon assuming a position as a junior executive in an international division team of two, no advice, much less guidance, was offered to me on working with alien societies. It was my own father who instructed me with a singular guidance phrase. He told me that "international business is organized friendship." It was my associates around the world that provided me with a real practical cross-cultural indoctrination. I vividly recall the start of a meeting with a foreign distributor for my company who gently prodded me saying "I know you Americans are fond of getting down to business quickly but let us first get to know each other and build a trusting relationship." During my international executive tenure I must have engaged in hundreds of negotiation sessions resulting in the drafting and execution of distributor agreements, licensing and franchising contracts, as well as direct foreign investment arrangements in the creation of joint ventures and offshore subsidiaries. I dealt with global suppliers and international carriers, cross-territorial retail chains, and a host of lawyers from numerous nations. While being professionally trained as a lawyer with accounting experience at Price Waterhouse & Co., not once in my global managerial responsibilities did any of the volumes of concluded agreements result in a legal suit or even the threat of one. Every potential disagreement or perceived violation was settled amicably because I learned to practice what my father told me. Create relationships and the rest will follow. It wasn't until I started teaching that all of my prior experiences came into focus and I recognized the prime importance of a cross-cultural education. The learning provided me in the field was now being codified and explained in more formalized theoretical principles. What I witnessed was now given a defined instructional basis and as I reflected back I began to understand my personal cultural traits as well as those I had previously dealt with.

While this book was written for international managers, it has equal relevance to society as a whole, as an examination into cross-determinants to define and explain the influence of culture on our lives as generated under the auspices of commercial dealings can help promote a rapprochement to the social forces that tend to separate us. It is only through a cross-cultural education that the veils of secrecy are drawn open allowing varying societies to see that to a certain degree we are more alike than different. We all possess both sides of the cultural determinants that define and therefore control our values, inspire our motivational drives, and influence our prejudicial perceptions of others. Cross-territorial trade, the commercial imperative, historically and today, is the prime activity of human beings that brings us into contact with diverging cultures fostering. It follows that on such a platform a greater cross-cultural understanding and appreciation can be constructed. The use of cultural determinants based on the research emanating from an inspection into international business organizations and their global relationships is therefore a valuable pedagogy not just for managers of such institutions but for divergent worldwide societies.

As a practitioner in the real commercial world, my tenure as an international executive, and later in life as a professor of international business, I have always harbored the thought that while the practice of business has often been a maligned profession and never treated as a science, a lot could be learned from applying some of the research the cross-territorial trade process has generated in a wider social context. Dealing with others and establishing relationships is at the core of the commercial imperative, and at the same time life. As I traveled the world meeting and working with a diversity of business associates the relationships I formed with numerous varied culturally indoctrinated societies changed me. On every overseas trip, I arrived as one person and left as another. It was and still is for me a continuing learning experience.

Cross-territorial trade culminating in today's modern globalization imperative requires one to engage others who are different from us and as such an education in the culture of ourselves and others is the prime requirement for success. Today's managers need to gain a global prospective in order to enhance their professional credentials and be able to forge partnerships and relationships within an integrated commercial world. They need to broaden their insights into how different societies think, what they value, and how they are motivated.

In an academic structure the teaching of cross-cultural theoretical approaches to understand and appreciate societal differences to enable potential managers to function successfully in our globalized commercial world is evidenced by course changes and certificate additions in major universities. Columbia University, advertising the benefits of its School of Continuing Education, encourages students to take on the world's evolving challenges by mastering the world's emerging professions via graduate programs in strategic communication and practice as well as negotiation and conflict resolution in a global environment; in essence a cross-cultural education element. In an interview the new dean of Harvard Business School, Nitin Nohria discusses three new components to their curriculum. Two of them are culturally driven: (1) a new leadership quality he calls emotional intelligence—being smart about your own emotions and the emotions of others and (2) globalization—acquiring greater savvy about what is going on in the world.[1]

This noted direction brought home my father's words again, that business is organized friendship, knowing yourself and others, their mind-sets and the environment both you and they live in. I kept thinking what lessons from assessing culturally driven value determinants investigated from a commercial viewpoint could be used to create a bridge between East and West. Is there a prime factor that on the face separates us but upon further inspection and reflected analysis can be used to draw us together? I think so, and such is the underlying theme of this book.

Finding methods to bring cross-cultural awareness into the diverging commercial world practicing globalization can also be used as a connecting rod for societies in general. I must candidly admit that my international executive experiences coupled with my university instructorship and research into globally induced business subjects have been influenced by the words of Socrates, the Greek philosopher (469 BC to 399 BC) writing in *Plutarch, Of Banishment*, proclaiming "I am not an Athenian or a Greek, but a citizen of the world." The commercial managers of today as well as students wanting to undertake such a career must understand and be appreciative of this simple consideration. In doing so, one is compelled to reflect on one's own culture and those of others; and such is the intention of this book.

Perhaps a good example of applying the Socrates quote to the business world of today comes from the simply stated title of a new book by authors Cabrera and Unruh, *Being Global.*[2] It is a refreshing reference as opposed to the titles of most books on culture which include the adjective word cross, often hyphenated, to produce the term cross-culture. This applied terminology supposedly emerged in the social sciences arena in the 1930s as the result of research done by George Murdock, a Yale University anthropologist labeling his investigative results based on statistical compilations of cultural data as a cross-cultural survey.

The use of cross in conjunction with culture to denote no less define the subject matter, the relationship between alternating societies, contains both a negative and a positive grammatical connotation. The perceptual inference most attributed to the term results in an acuity of contrary forces, an unfavorable or irritated condition. An intersection, in the physical sense, of opposing ideas or being at cross purposes. A conflict of diverging cultures and a potential negative state. However an alternative depiction of the term can mean an involving and intersecting union. To transverse reciprocally wherein the resulting unified entity is strengthened and not weakened by the merger. It is this positive approach to the artificially created word, cross-culture, that I believe is the true subjective interpretation and its hopeful objective usage.

I have benefited greatly from my business associates around the world whose patience in educating a cultural novice will never be forgotten.

This book differs from the multitude of conscientious well-presented textbooks and guides on cross-cultural inspection. While using basic research developed pedagogical approaches by learned researchers I have incorporated additional references across a number of other scholarly disciplines as well as those squarely outside of the academic field of cultural anthropology. Literature, as well as other artistic works, has always commented on mankind's philosophical relationships with one another, and even if such materials may not be grounded in scientifically accepted principles they offer valuable insights on how we see ourselves and others; the cultural imperative.

Velo in the Preface of her book[3] references a weblog quote of renowned cross-cultural researcher Geert Hofstede posting, "Culture is more often a source of conflict then of synergy. Cultural differences are a nuisance at best and often a disaster." This definition as applied to cultural variances positions it as an irritation, an offensive annoying interloper in the affairs of people that conceivably prevents, as Hofstede indicates, smooth and efficient transactions between and amongst opposing social groups. Such depiction of cultural differences therefore carries a negative connotation. On the other hand, author Velo, who basically agrees with the Hofstede comment, offers a most salient counterpoint. She portrays cultural differences as a source of creativity, positioning them as a "continuous challenge to the boundaries of our thought" thereby acting as a catalyst for "inspiration and understanding." Such a positive approach to the irritation caused by encountering alien cultures is a most refreshing reflection on the subject, as in essence she is stating that allowing for different approaches, seeing things from the perspective of others or simply allowing for another opinion is a good not a bad idea. It can lead one to either the alteration of one's original thinking or it can cause one to more deeply inspect, the challenge factor, their own contentions and in the end strengthen it. Author Moua explores the positive application of culturally intelligent leadership (CIL) as a strategic skill set for managers, as it creates greater awareness, increases knowledge, and teaches patience; prime attributes in this ever growing diversified global business world.[4]

As I write these comments I must share with the reader my horoscope for March 23, 2012. Under Sagittarius (Nov. 22–Dec. 21) it reads "Differences in culture will cause you to think beyond the structures of your known world."[5] This aspiration is always a good positive direction not just for me but for all as it makes for better people and produces more informed capable international managers. As Harris concludes in the *Womb of Space* "cultural heterogeneity or cross-cultural capacity" provides an "evolutionary thrust" to the imagination.[6] He is echoing the sentiments of Velo on cross-cultural exposure, it expands our intellectual reach. It follows that any educational training offered on cross-cultural integration is not so much about acquiring skills to deal with people who are different from you, the ability to manipulate them. It is about learning from them in order to improve yourself. Most readers are familiar with the refrain "think outside the box." The phrase implores one to go beyond their normal boundaries of understanding, to think differently. An intercultural indoctrination goes further. It allows one to turn the proverbial box over, dump out its contents and refill it with a wider and more in depth spectrum of knowledgeas gleaned from exposure to another culture.

It is these proactive affirmative valued uses of a cross-cultural indoctrination along with my own experiences that motivated and inspired this book.

I am indebted to David Parker, publisher of Business Expert Press for his constant encouragement and production liaison Cindy Durand for her guidance. I remain respectfully grateful to the International Collection Editors, Professors S. Tamer Cavusgil, Michael Czinkota, and Gary Knight for their thoughtful comments and suggestions. Let me also thank the team at Exeter Premedia Service in India for their copyediting and editorial proofreading, a testament to the global community we all live and work in.

The book is dedicated to my grandchildren, Alex, Josh, Brady, Addison, Kendall, Isaac, and Liam. May they live in a world that respects diversity while embracing similarity; coming to realize, as I have, that we are all more the same than different. May their lives be built on what we all share and not what separates us.

Introduction

It's mid-October 2011 and I am in the process of editing this book so a portion of my mind is always focused on the subject of culture. I find myself with my wife waiting on the grounds of Dingeman Elementary School, part of the San Diego Unified School District, to have lunch with our grandson. We always look forward to this special time with Brady who is 6, although he reminds me he is really 6¾, a first grader at the school. We join him as his class marches in unison out of the room. The numerous differences in their facial and physical stature depict a wide variance in ethnic and racial characteristics. We are witnessing a mini parade of delegates who could be attending a universal world conference. As this is picture day all his friends are dressed nicely but we notice that many of them are clothed in garments adorned with textures and remnants that seem to depict an artful indication, as exemplified by colors and embroidery, of their individual cultural heritage. While the dress of each child stands out from the other it is a common purpose, the mutual excitement of picture day, a shared collective agenda that stands out. We follow along to the outdoor tented table area where many children either unload their home packed lunches or buy the daily offering.

As I look around the assembly of first and second graders I cannot help but again take note of the wide variances in the assembly before me. It seems that almost every overt racial, ethnic, or nationally identifiable group is represented. But the kids don't sit or mingle in specifically particular cultural groups. All are mixed with each other, smiling, laughing, and talking at once as the food somehow makes its way into their mouths. As a special treat we bought Brady Japanese sushi. While some are eating pizza, the school dish of the day, others chomp down on bologna and PBJ (peanut butter and jelly) sandwiches, yogurt, veggies, and fruit snacks. Still others have rice bowls and tamales while some grab hard to distinguish substances from plastic containers. Many are sharing their meals but amid the chaos all just seem to be enjoying themselves.

As the meals are finished they make their way, and we tag along, to a large recreational park like area. Everyone is playing with everyone else with a spirit of fun and exuberance only childhood can exhibit. They calmly wait behind one another to cross the monkey bars, go down the slides, and get on swings. They form circles to play kick ball and tag, and share, passing to each other as they finish using them, jump ropes and hula hoops. My grandson introduces us to a slew of kids without the slightest inflection of stereotype labels or self-scribed prejudices—they are just his friends. They all get along and form relationships without the aid of a course or textbook much less training on cross-cultural issues. Without any specific prodding they all respect each other's diversity while embracing and relishing mutually shared activities.

The school stresses a fundamental learning grid built on personal skill development within a collaterally induced social environment. All the required mechanics, the traditional 3Rs, reading, writing, and arithmetic to advance comprehension are placed within this dual context. It consists of a balance of individualism and collectivism; a simple basic premise that both advances and solidifies cross-cultural interaction. I cannot help but reflect on this lesson.

As we grow up and leave our childhood behind, moving into the adult diversified world, things just get too complex; but do they have to? The observations at my grandson's school reminded me of a much earlier incident concerning my own children in a true cross-cultural environment. At the ages of 2 and 3 we took our son and daughter to the southern Caribbean island of Curacao, part of the Netherlands Antilles chain. As we sat them on the beach to play they were unexpectedly joined by three other young children around the same age. We later learned, when their respective parents came to pick them up, that one was from neighboring Venezuela, another from Holland, and the third a locally born toddler. The only commonality amongst these five infants was their attire; they all wore diapers and nothing else. Their native languages, even given their limited communication skills, ranged from Spanish to Dutch to Papiamentu, an island slang, and of course English. Recalling my eavesdropping on this group of children at play I was, and still am, amazed by their reverential interaction. They shared their toys, pails and shovels, plastic spoons, and shape making plastic sand impressions. They helped each other dig holes and carry water from the ocean to fill them. When one slipped over a mound another offered their hand to raise them. They jabbered between themselves, exchanging both reassuring and at times slightly disapproving glances even when misplaced steps caused sand to fall upon others' creative efforts. Mostly, however, they laughed and smiled, enjoying each other's company as they played in unison and sometimes alone. They accomplished collective tasks but they also paused to see how the others functioned individually. Mutual respect and admiration flowed as diversity prevailed. As observers they were building on what they shared. Any personal differences between them acted as part of a positive learning curve and not the negative connotation that often affects us as adults.

Some may argue that these two instances of cross-cultural exchange are merely examples of childhood innocence or naiveté; and they would be right. Culture, as defined and explored further in chapter 1, develops from a series of shared learned socially induced indoctrinations. Young children are yet to build an identifiable, much less codified cultural profile. They have to be taught such as best summarized by the lyrics and music contained in the song "You've Got To Be Carefully Taught" from the Tony and Pulitzer winning Broadway musical *South Pacific*.[1] The song's words tells us that you have to be "taught to hate and fear," to be scared "of people whose eyes are oddly made" and "whose skin is a different shade," concluding with the thought that one has to fear "all the people your relatives hate," "before you are 6 or 7 or 8." Young children begin life by sharing what they have in common per the examples previously presented and are taught later to be wary of differences. This is one of the prime problems with teaching cross-cultural matters to adult students and managers, they are already complicated creatures who have been taught to concentrate on differences. The first step may be to unlearn the perceptions, prejudices, and to a degree the beliefs that one's cultural education has instilled in them and aim to establish a cleaner mind-set slate. Create an environment of openness, that young children possess, as opposed to a semiclosed consciousness that sees things in black and white absolute images. All too often textbooks and guides on cross-cultural matter introduce the subject via a series of collections, value determinants, that highlight differences. By doing so, previously taught differential prejudices tend to be reinforced as opposed to concentrating on the ability to relearn from them in order to form positive results, what we all share.

For the average student, as well as a commercial manager receiving an introduction to cross-cultural appreciation and understanding the encountered social territory takes one on a complex journey across and between alternating cultures. The cultural matrix is constructed like the proverbial maze. It is not a straight line but a pathway of intersecting exits that always lead to new confusing theoretical definitions. It moves through countless levels of introspections and at each new intersection again splits off into ever increasing subsections that are too often portrayed as standing on their own. This is because the study of culture has been visited from so many angles that when they are placed in an educational kaleidoscope they are seen as a brilliant collection of multicolored lights that while dazzling the viewer do not provide any qualifying direction for the real world. Plus, with each turn or adjustment of such a cultural instrument, a new array of designs or systems of inspection is produced.

It is difficult to attain a narrow focus that would afford the interested observer, no less the managerial student desirous of securing a practical working knowledge, a concise understanding of how to apply what they are taught. Numerous collections devoted to cultural determinants by various researchers and theorists investigating mankind's social relationships as well as values and belief systems to resolve the problems of life appear in countless texts and articles. Many of these approaches stem from observations and examinations of the commercial environmental world as the process of trade is the most universal of all human activities.

In the modern era of globalization the ability to master the skills of cross-cultural understanding and its application are of paramount importance to international managers. With the massive growth of multinational organizations the ability to strategize, manage, and form working substantive associations with alien societies is central to success. The problem with obtaining, much less acquiring a useful knowledge to allow one to properly navigate across and between cultural differences, is that so many components are thrown into the mix that students and managers become both disillusioned and confused. Those studying or being trained in the art of cross-cultural assimilation are therefore prone to precharacterize or catalog the anticipated behaviors of alien cultures they will be engaging; a dangerous assumption at best. Often this process places societies in neat tidy dimensional patterns portraying them as adapting or representing one side of a cultural determinant to the exclusion of its opposite characteristic. There seems to be a pedagogy that stresses memorization over guided observation when the real purpose of cross-cultural education is to expand the mind, not fill it with facts. This book will show that: (1) all cultures possess both sides of culturally induced variables and the measurement degrees separating them are relevant in appreciating and navigating differences by concentrating on similarities, (2) the multitude of research oriented cultural determinant collections can be filtered and reduced to a workable few fundamental applications which can be further condensed to a core or central cultural determinant that controls or influences all the others; the interplay of individualism and collectivism.

Maybe it's time to get back to the simplistic lessons of elementary school and invoke the human commonality we all shared as children while retaining our individuality. It would seem that as we move from adolescence into adulthood the uncomplicated cultural similarities are socialized out of us. What we share is greater than what separates us, and such should be the main bridge to cross the global cultural abyss.

The Cultural Jungle Questionnaire

Perhaps the best way to exemplify the complicated study of culture is offered by the following list of questions:

1. How do you put a giraffe into a refrigerator?
   STOP AND THINK ABOUT THIS BEFORE LOOKING AT THE RIGHT ANSWER
   The correct answer is: *Open the refrigerator, put in the giraffe, and close the door.* The problem is that in the study of culture there is a pronounced tendency to overly complicate the issue with numerous indoctrinations that confuse and obscure the simplest approach.
2. How do you put an elephant into a refrigerator?

DID YOU SAY, open the refrigerator, put in the elephant and close the door? Wrong answer.

The correct answer: *Open the refrigerator, take out the giraffe, put in the elephant, and close the door.* The secondary issue is that culture is acquired as it proceeds on a series of learned developmental steps or platforms moving from one to another; and you cannot jump ahead. Each step enables one to proceed to the next.

3. The Lion King is hosting an animal conference in the jungle. All the animals attend...except one. Which one does not attend?

DIFFICULT? NOT REALLY.

The correct answer: *The elephant.* You already put him in the refrigerator and closed the door as learned in question 2, so he cannot attend. This is the third facet of cultural understanding; all aspects of cultural development interface with each other and cannot be used alone, settling on a singular step, as the answer to cross-cultural engagements. Culture is multifaceted and one needs to respect all that has transpired before.

4. There is a river in the jungle you must cross but it is used by crocodiles and you do not have a boat or raft. How do you manage getting across?

PROBLEMATIC?

The correct answer: *You jump into the river and swim across.* All the animals, including the crocodiles, are attending the Lion King's animal conference so they won't bother you as you swim across the river. This last question exemplifies cultural appreciation as even when an issue is presented that seems to be, on its face, not connected with a decidedly discernible cultural linkage, the approach to be taken can contain a valued cultural component. Simply put, everything happens in the context of cultural overtones.

The Cultural Minutiae Syndrome

Although placed within the general context of cultural anthropology, the wide spectrum of information given in most educational forums, from academic institutions to cross-cultural training sessions, is therefore problematic. Beyond the perfunctory questions what is culture and how does it evolve, a presentation on its component roots, the subject has been approached from numerous theoretical applications themselves based on numerous scientifically related research disciplines. It is treated with theoretically generated dimensions, context-based definitions, generic characteristics, and geographical clusters along with a host of classification designations

The research into the field continues to expand with countless books, journal articles, Internet sites, and blogs devoted to the subject matter. Academic conferences feature cross-cultural seminars while a whole new business service component, cross-cultural training, is offered by consulting organizations. Every textbook on international business, approached from any discipline, provides a chapter on the effect of culture on this prime branch of learning as business school curriculums have been reengineered in recognition of its importance as an important tool in managerial skill development. The recent focus on ethical conduct of business organizations, especially the conduct of multinational firms, includes a cultural element to help navigate ethical dilemmas faced by the increasing cross-border operational reach of such institutions.

The expansion and concentration afforded the subject matter is to be welcomed, and therefore supported as a worthwhile endeavor, but it may be time to provide those being indoctrinated into this most influential factor in life—how we conduct ourselves with others—a more practical simplified approach. It is the inspectional theme of this book to propose such a direction and as such it could be called a *theory of everything (sort of)*.[2]

This book uses the commonly shared culture of trade as the wedge to open the dam separating the proverbial East and West divide, a colloquial expression for worldwide cultural differences. Patches of common ground can be found in the cross-territorial trade imperative. It can act as a platform of connectivity to facilitate a dialog of understanding of what really causes the abyss to form, and hence find the key to bridge the disconnect. Economic life and human life are connected as one sustains the other. From the lessons of trade did the world learn how to form relationships with one another. Via an analysis into cultural differences through the investigatory lens of the commercial process can real steps be taken to ease tensions and facilitate cross-cultural improvement.

Economic activities are embedded in the establishment of a series of social relationships as the process of exchange mirrors society's values and attitudes. Such inspection offers a realistic insight into how people differ in the construction and implementation of life's choices; the cultural imperative.

The Global Cross-Cultural Divide

"Oh, East is East, and West is West, and never the twain shall meet" is a refrain from a collection of ballads by R. Kipling based on the experiences of English soldiers dispatched at the end of the 1800s around the world to defend the social imperialistic and economically directed mercantile policies of the British Empire.[3] The phrase reflects not only the emotional reaction of those posted to alien environments during this period but also serves as a symbolic reference to the chasm between East and West societies that have historically existed and continues today. In the modern era, this divide, as evidenced by variances in sociopolitical and economic principles, and fueled by differences in religious and philosophical ideologies, seems only to grow larger leading to more troublesome conflicts. It would seem that the world is being asked to make a choice. It reminds one of the lyric "East is east and west is west And the wrong one I have chose" from the song *Buttons and Bows* which first appeared in the Bob Hope and Jane Russell film, *The Paleface* (1948) and won the Academy Award for Best Original Song.[4] Today the dialog continues. It is the subject of numerous publications while permeating the communication airwaves via commentaries on the radio, television, and the Internet. From political aspirants to the agenda driven propagandas of public groups the debate over the direction of the world based on cultural induced differences between the East and West rages. Outside the political and religious groups striving to be heard on the issue the business community have been pulled into the discussion. Multinational companies are often depicted as the benefactors of globalization and hence potential players in the so-called unfinism known as the East–West game. In order to avoid a collision of opposing culturally induced mind-sets, depicted above as East versus West but in reality running across all geographical regions, that might force the world to decide which system will dominate requires a better appreciation and understanding of cultural differences. Beyond its practical application in cross-cultural business venturing if we are to counter the possibility of future global confrontations we must begin to explore the intellectual underpinnings of what separates us. A design of cultural partnership as opposed to cultural division is proposed and it is constructed on the foundation of commercial activities.

A Geographical or Mind-Set Split?

The commonly used directional or geographical characterization of the world's population refers to an artificially constructed demarcation line called East and West. As such it is difficult to precisely calculate with absolute certainty where the two sides actually diverge and go their separate distinctive way. The normal accepted definition places the European continent coupled with the Western Hemisphere on one side and the land beginning at Istanbul, Turkey and moving both east across the Asian continent and south to the Middle East weaving its way into Africa, circling back West across the continent on the other. In *Myths To Live By*, Campbell introduces his chapter titled "The Separation of East and West" by offering his own definition:

> I draw the main line dividing Orient from Occident vertically through Iran, along a longitude about 60 degrees east of Greenwich. This can be thought of as a cultural watershed. Eastward of the line there are two creative high-culture matrices: India and the Far East (China and Japan); and westward, likewise, there are two: the Levant or Near East, and Europe. In their mythologies, religions, philosophies, and ideals, no less than in their styles of life, dress and in their arts, these four domains have remained throughout their histories distinct. And yet they do group significantly in two orders of two: India and the Far East, on one hand; the Levant and Europe, on the other hand.[5]

But in reality the East–West demographic is a culturally induced mind-set. It is not a set of longitudes and latitudes on a map. In the modern era of not only commercial globalization but social globalization a more borderless world has emerged. After the First World War, nations were beset with population shifts and cross-immigration so that the historic geographical definition of East and West is today more blurred. What remains is not a series of connecting points on the globe but the meandering of people across the globe taking their cultural heritage with them. One is apt to meet an Indian on the streets of New York City, who still thinks and acts like he was still crossing a New Delhi intersection. Just like an American cutting through a narrow 1000-year-old alleyway in Beijing on his way to enjoy a lunch of diemsong with his Chinese friends the physical environment may change but the underlying mindset remains.

Other writers have described the cultural gap between societies as a clash of the Old and New Worlds, especially after the era of European global exploration and discovery as begun by Christopher Columbus. The fact that people at such times lived on separate and distinct continents with vast differences in ecosystems produced deep variances in societal attitudes, beliefs, and behavior influenced value systems. Their fates however, since that period and continuing today, have and will be bound together for better or worse.[6] In fact, geographically speaking, as one travels West they end up in the East (the Columbus directive) and vice versa. In the end, we are all connected and the inherent duality of presumed opposites as part of the whole emerges.

A Socioeconomic Link

In *The Ancient Economy*, M. Finley argued that culturally engineered social status and civic ideology as opposed to the laws of supply and demand controlled economic decision-making and commercial imperative in the ancient economies as exemplified by the Greco-Roman era.[7] In essence, Finley theorizes that economics cannot be separated from social relationships which are controlled by culturally inspired value determinants. The simple conclusion is that economics is a good inspection tool to allow one to not only visualize but also measure and quantify culturally inspired differences between social groups. Studying how people satisfy their need production—their activities in the process of exchange and therefore distribution of goods required for the chief purpose of securing life and/or procuring a better life well exemplifies the mind-sets of people. People satisfy their private needs in a communal context and it is this dichotomy, the interplay of individualism and collectivism, that forms the basis of cultural inspection. Early merchants were the first cross-territorial ambassadors and therefore the first practitioners of the art of cross-cultural exchange.

Classical economics defines a free market as opportunity costs—the necessity of making difficult choices between competing goods. Substitute competing cultures for goods and an examination into how we can use the exchange system to foster social cooperation emerges. This pedagogical direction may help to unlock the stalemate that has and continues to block the blending of East and West value determinants.

Nancy Koehn in her review of *Economics of Good and Evil* by Sedlacek writes that the Czech author aims to humanize the most powerful of the social sciences, economics, concluding that "As sophisticated and mathematical as economics has become, it is ultimately a cultural phenomenon."[8] Koehn cites Sedlacek stating that "Economics should mean the art of helmsmanship" acquainting this science with the management of people and resources within a political social environment, a concept echoed in chapter 3 by the earlier Greek philosophers who coined the term economics.

The traditional East–West dichotomy as a descriptive phrase is used by economic historians Morris in *Why the West Rules—For Now*[9] and Ferguson in *Civilization, The West and the Rest*.[10] Both researchers describe events in these respective split geographical regions to explain the pre-eminence and then fall of the East as opposed to the emergence and dominance of the West beginning in the 14th century and continuing into present times but questionable for the future. While numerous theoretical inquiries are offered by both authors, based on their separate development of social institutions to political, economic, and philosophical conditions, they rarely qualify such differences using a cultural imperative. Morris refers to social development, the growth of civilization, as "basically, a group's ability to master its physical and intellectual environment to get things done. A bundle of technological, subsistence, organizational, and cultural accomplishments through which people feed, cloth, house and reproduce themselves."[11] In essence, he is describing, as latter presented in chapter 1, the definition of culture—how mankind handles and assigns value choices to their lives. Ferguson also alludes to the cultural element when he states that "The West, then, is much more than just a geographical expression. It is a set of norms, behaviors and institutions with borders that are blurred in the extreme. The implications of that are worth pondering."[12] He is really asking the reader to consider, in his words "ponder," the underlying building block of the East–West transitional phenomenon, cultural considerations. He even notes the 1915 comment of German sociologist Max Weber in *Confucianism and Taoism* defining Eastern ways of life as based on "Confucian rationalism as meaning 'rational adjustment to the world," as opposed to the Western concept of 'rational mastery of the world'."[13] This reference to mankind's orientation to nature, as either subjugation to, in harmony with, or control over, is part of the series of culture determinants offered by one of the first researchers in the field, Florence Kluckhohn as presented in chapter 3.

Ferguson depicts the ability of the West to leap ahead over the East as based on six applications; namely, competition, science, the rule of law regarding private property, medicine, consumerism, and work ethic, that such applications embraced by the West and dismissed or constrained by the East allowed for civilization to emerge more quickly in one region of the globe to the detriment of the other. Four of these fortuitous advantages are traceable to cultural differences with the base element individualism versus collectivism influencing their emergence. Beginning with competition, Ferguson notes that intra-European rivalries and the desire to break the lock on the Eastern spice trade inspired the age of exploration by Western regional states to ensure their separate economic and political well being. Starting with the 1492 voyage of Christopher Columbus sailing West and Vasco de Gama in 1497 to round the Cape of Good Hope and proceed to India did the competitive initiative give the West an advantage over the East. He contrasts such motivational desire with the hold placed on Chinese venturing, technically a royal ban, after the Star Fleet in 1424 returned from its exhaustive travels that took it to India and Africa. This decision exemplified Confucian philosophy, as noted above, to promote harmony by adjusting to the world and not challenging it; that stability as opposed to change aids the common good. Such differences between the West and the East have at their core a cultural component; individualism versus collectivism.

Individualistic cultures are ingrained with an initiative to challenge, compete, and embrace change as the bringer of improvement. Collective societies view competition as leading to the unbalancing and disharmony of the cooperative nature of the group with change to be accepted passively lest it upset the status quo. Another of Ferguson's concepts that propelled the West over the East is the rule of law as expressed in the inviolability of individual freedom as demonstrated by secured private property rights protected by a representative government. He recounts the rise of individual freedom in Europe via the breakdown of a sovereign power beginning with the English Magna Carta and the dispersal of authority into the hands of nobles, and then to municipalities, all leading to its more progressive form in the establishment of the United States and its strong constitution protective of individual rights. In the East, however, such reforms did not materialize. The Kingdoms in China and Japan, although supported by nobles, did not break the chain of absolute control by the centralized monarchies. To challenge such authority would be to upset the collective good of the people, as the Emperors, by owning all material property, looked out for the common masses. This is another example of individualism versus collectivism as the prime influential agent in how societies operate.

The development of a consumer society and the Protestant work ethic are also cited as contributing to the mastery of the West over the East. Both concepts are indicative of individualistic initiative and choice trumping the collective stagnation of group passive acceptance. Although Ferguson does not specifically assign culture the status it deserves as a prime stimulant for the emergence of such applications he does attribute the usage of culture to produce varying results by there different Western societies. In his chapter on property rights, the colonization of the Americas, he takes "two Western cultures," the British in the North and the Spanish and Portuguese in the South and shows how their export and imposition of their individual cultures on peoples and lands created different outcomes.[14]

Both these learned authors, Morris and Ferguson, in characterizing East–West societal development need to inject a stronger cultural component into the respective analysis they attach to the historical events depicted in their talented narratives. The cultural differences inherent in each of their geographical regions were a contributory if not underlying force in the conclusions they reach.

Cultural Layering

Culture is often compared to an onion with its many overlaying layers forming the whole. Peeling them off one by one is a tiresome, troubling procedure, more so stopping to examine each sheet or leaf. Imagine if one had to reassemble the discarded pieces correlating them in the process to understand how they fit together, an even more difficult task. But countless researchers have offered lists, in essence layers, of cultural determinants to explain how we think and act toward one another. If one applies, as proposed and applied in chapter 5, the principle of Occam's Razor that allows one to cut though the theoretical minutiae and arrive at simplified singular and core controlling determinant then the differences can be examined and clarified. In essence, splitting the onion in half preserves the whole but lets one see the layered content in its ordered fashion. At the center, as this book postulates and attempts to show, is collectivism versus individualism. Both cultural variances inhabit the same human condition, acting as a balancing Yin and Yang of our physic. Therefore each culture has elements of these two opposing directives.

However, one side or the other acts as the primary directive of our mental value determinant influencing our behavior—how we think and how we react; and gives rise to all the other derivatives, collateral inspired value determinants. Individualism and collectivism comprise the fundamental cultural value determinant and act as society's chief controlling agent. Its influence on the mind-set of man can be traced back to antiquity as mankind banded together for their personal survival. The merged degree of the individual into a group was and still is the prime motivator of mankind. As expressed in the words of John Lennon "come together right now, over me"[15] well exemplifies this primeval imperative. How we approach this task defines a culture. Each society harbors the prime competing forces of individualism and collectivism. As both components exist in all of us, the duality factor, there exists the potential to saddle cross-cultural similarities and promote cultural unity.

SECTION 1

The Basics of Culture

CHAPTER 1

What Is Culture, Where Does It Come From?

Culture is the core determinant of all we are. It is the filter of our senses and therefore the chief controlling agent of life's values, its perceptions, and decisions. Inspection to determine how and why people act the way they do is a far ranging field of learning. Housed in the arena of sociology and psychology the scientific discipline of anthropology studies humans across two interlinked scopes of inquiry—history and geography. The field is divided into four distinct but related subfields that impact, borrow, and therefore influence each other. They are:

1. *archaeology*: studying ancient and prehistoric societies;
2. *physical anthropology*: examining the biological make-up of human beings;
3. *anthropological linguistics*: a comparative inquiry into languages and communication;
4. *cultural anthropology*: the search for similarities and differences among contemporary peoples of the world.

Cultural anthropology looks to identify and describe how people's thought processes produce a set of values upon which they construct their life, the choices they make, and the actions undertaken driven by varied mind-sets. While the world shares many similarities, it differs in many others. There is a marked tendency to assume that we are all alike, for example, in terms of basic human nature. This comes from the fact that most of us draw such conclusions from our limited observations of the immediate society around us. When confronted with an alien or foreign society whose people act differently from us, we think of them as weird, strange, or exhibiting downright wrong behavior. Culture is not positive or negative, it just exists. It is our judgments of culture that contain such judicial dispositions.

Our assumptions of reality are culturally bound because we practice cultural monotheism. This natural tendency disqualifies all of us to act as empathetic arbitrators of differences as we are all strongly anchored in and held back by the chains of our own culture. To unlock this judgmental stranglehold one needs to embrace the idea that cultural pluralism, in masked form, resides in all of us. We possess, although hidden from our consciousness, dormant cultural traits that mirror to an extent those people who on the surface are perceived as different from us, and vice versa—what is called the duality factor.

Exploring the Meaning of Culture

When one thinks of culture, a mirage of defining terms and examples appears. To be "cultured" is to have received an introduction to the classy things in life. We often think one who is cultured possesses a superior education or at least an awareness of such things as the fine arts and classical literature, is knowledgeable about the philosophies of great teachers, and appreciative of the music of the great masters.

When describing the culture of a society, we normally address surface attributes—those characteristics that we can physically sense as stimulating our eyes, ears, smell, and touch. But below the illustrated surface or *folk culture* lies a host of hidden or *deep cultural* attributes. They are recessed in the mind-sets of people, exercising control over their thoughts and behavior and are responsible for their core beliefs and values—how people rationalize and think. Figure 1.1 illustrates the multisurface aspects of the cultural minutiae. Like an iceberg, most of a group's perceived cultural attitudes, the overt, lie on the top layer while those below the surface, the covert, are revealed only when people are engaged in relationships with others and the curtain of familiarity is drawn.

Even our own cultural knowledge of ourselves is often masked as rarely does one take the time to examine, much less classify one's personal tendencies, why we behave and act in a certain way. Our deep cultural identity is only challenged when we encounter an alien society and begin to perhaps question our own values in the face of differences.

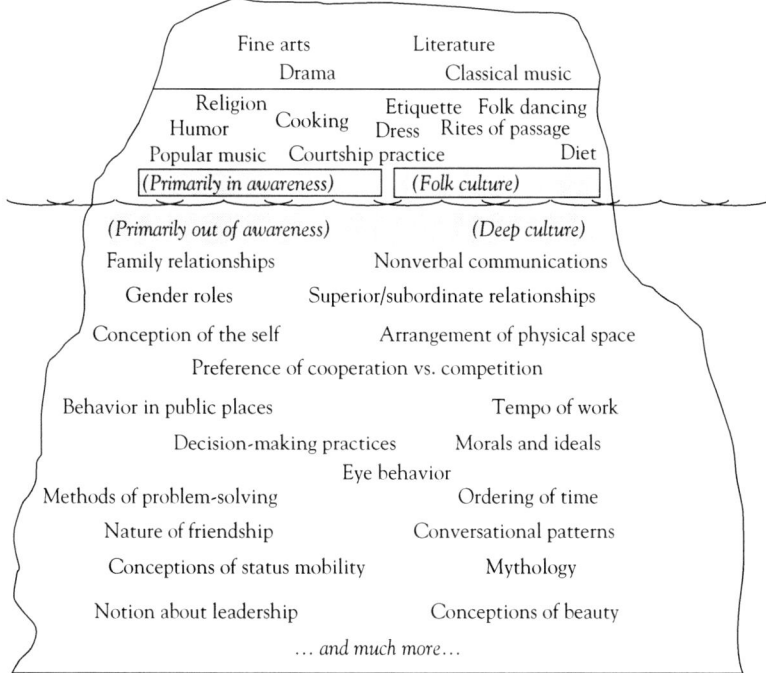

Figure 1.1. The cultural iceberg.

Defining Culture

There may be no single acceptable definition of what is meant by the all encompassing term culture. In his book *The Cultural Dimension of International Business*, Gary Ferraro notes that two early researchers in the field "A. L. Kroeber and Clyde Kluckhohn in 1952 identified more than 160 different definitions of culture."[1] In its simplest description culture is a design system for living. Edward Tylor, writing over a century ago, described culture as "that complex whole which includes knowledge, belief, art, morals, law, custom and any other capabilities and habits acquired by man as a member of society."[2] M. J. Herskovits depicted culture as mental, "the man made part of the environment" as opposed to the material or physical created by nature.[3] Geert Hofstede referred to the process as the "collective programming of the mind which distinguishes the members of one group from another."[4] Hofstede described a series of habitual thinking patterns made up of shared values, beliefs, symbols, behaviors, and assumptions that define the group. Technically, culture is an abstraction that cannot be seen or touched, an intangible mental process that Hofstede further defines as an intellectual system to help people solve problems. But it is reflected in one's activities, so it produces material examples, physically observable tangible elements from artifacts to language—the surface or above water aspects of the cultural iceberg (see Figure 1.1). In the end, culture is most vividly expressed through the values it produces in people and is exemplified by what people do and do not do in a given society—that which is considered as acceptable behavior and that which is deemed unacceptable behavior. Prevailing or dominant actions and/or reactions to life are regarded as conventional and tend to be classified to describe the culture of a given group.

It is important to remember this point when examining all these approaches to the subject of culture, as the word "collective" refers to the fact that it is contingent on the combined reflections of the members of a specific group. Hence culture is shared by two or more individuals and is indicative of their repetitive, normative, demonstrative, and therefore expected patterns of behavior—allowing one to qualify these as a deductive generalized characterization of a society. However, this consideration is both positive and negative. If we can classify a specific culture via a set of applied research-based determinants, those of oneself and others, we may learn in advance how to form relationships with them, by concentrating on the similarities but keeping in mind the differences. On the other hand, such a classification approach induces prejudices, a prejudgment that may not allow for a cultural free space to exist where one first observes before forming opinions to guide their action and reaction. Edward T. Hall warns those studying culture that it often hides more that it reveals and what it obscures most effectively is an appreciation and understanding of one's own culture.[5] Culture can therefore be a minefield of contradictions, misplaced assumptions, false observations, and tainted conclusions but its value as a relationship building tool should not be dismissed or understated. One is instructed to just tread lightly in the illuminated path it provides. The numerous sets of cross-cultural determinants, as reviewed in chapter 3, can result in a labyrinth whose positive metaphorical intent is meant to hone one's focus and provide a pathway of understanding. But to many the vast collections turn into a maze, perverting the ability to comprehend, often confusing and trapping the cross-cultural traveler.

Where Does Culture Come From?

In the end, culture can be summarized as "everything that people have, think and do as members of their society"[6]; a total way of life. With representative examples of culture both above and below the surface of inspection and with defined parameters of what it is, it is valuable in understanding how it works to consider where it comes from. If culture is the sum total of one's observations and indoctrinations it follows that it is a learned experience that begins at birth. While the hardware of our brain is biologically constructed the loaded software is placed in the mental system by interaction via our sensory mechanisms with one's environment—the material world and relationships with its inhabitants. Unlike the genetic construction of the physical brain which is internal, cultural learning is external. This simple axiom is universal and while cultures differ around the world the process of acquiring culture is similarly reproduced in all societies.

Cultural indoctrination is the sum of all one is exposed to as we emerge from the womb, and hence it continues to death. During life it never stops. The process is composed of inputs beginning with the family unit and like the proverbial pebble thrown into a pond it radiates outward growing wider and wider as new segments of exposure are engaged. This mechanism of learning is socialization. It starts with family/kinship relationships conferring upon us our first introduction to our cultural heritage. It is influenced by the physical environment in which we live as we view how others who went before us have adapted to it. Our cultural identity is more formally built on the educational system one is placed in. It is molded on the ethical and moral teachings encountered in a society that morph into secular laws as well as spiritual guidance based on religious doctrines and philosophical approaches defining expected behavior. It is also prejudiced by unwritten customs and traditions that are followed. Hence one often hears the refrain "this just isn't done" or "this is how we do it" without pointing to a specific educational indoctrination or authoritative prescribed written code of conduct. While one's cultural programming includes formal and informal training it is absorbed from mere observation via general immersion in society as well as through trial and error as one is punished for unacceptable actions. It emerges from problem solving of everyday matters.

Cultural Steps: Levels of Associations Contributing to Cultural Self-Identity Building

Cultural indoctrination is a journey of steps or building levels that one goes through in a given society (see Figure 1.2). The first step is birthright cultural indoctrination initially acquired via the family one emerges from the womb or is adopted into. It is this first primary group that provides the initial level of cultural indoctrination and includes the collateral influence of a clan or tribe of common ethnic, racial, or religious/philosophical principles that the family resides in. This initial creation step in the development of one's cultural identity is itself based on a closed groups system of mating, marriage or its monogamous equivalent, child rearing, and family structure. Even within a uniform politically designated society such family orientations produce regional differences. All our basic assumptions are tethered like a life sustaining umbilical cord to this first level and this exposure tends to act as the anchor of our core values. The saying "it takes a village to bring up a child" is indicative of the surrounding geographical social arena, one's associations with others, that one grows in. It is also made up of one's climatic and physical environment as well as the socioeconomic and political exposure one encounters with a particular sovereign territory. As with family units even the norms and behaviors experienced with a given bordered nation may be further segregated by differences in domestic regional characteristics setting them apart from other citizens of the same nation.

While the nomenclature of culture is normally prescribed to identify the national culture of a particular geographical area of the world there are other influencing factors often denoted as subcultures as they are embedded in a country or regional territory. Two identifiable contributory components are educational/professional and organizational. Some would argue that these additional cultural steps are not a set of values but instead are merely a series of acceptable group practices imposed by the power channels of such institutional subgroups one associates with and hence are not a natural process of cultural assimilation.[7] However, as powerful stimulators of behavior and perceptual development they are part of the cultural building process. One's cultural path in life is further influenced by the structured choice of the formal education afforded them.

From primary or grade school up and through undergraduate university, masters, and perhaps even the doctorate level such scholastic exposures to specific instructional programs and curriculums chosen alter one's thinking matrix and cultural indoctrination. With some degrees culminating in acceptance into the professional ranks or a specialized field of study the endowments provided by one's academic experiences assist in the manifestation of selected cultural inputs.

At the top level is organizational culture. Organizational culture is a relatively new field in the arena of cultural anthropology with research in the area pioneered by studies of commercial institutions and managerial approaches to the internal psychology, attitudes, experiences, beliefs, and values of shared groups of people operating toward a unified goal. It is the goal orientation that defines and separates this category of culture, how things are accomplished, from the normative other levels of cultural development. Organizational culture can be simply stated as *the way things get done around here*.[8] It is reflective of a patterned activity of shared assumptions the group have evolved to solve problems. As such the paradigm created runs the gamut from mission values, the expectation or goal creator, to tangible control systems and structures while also containing influential emotion-based intangible elements such as institutional symbols, rituals, and routines as well as stories and myths, all working together to sustain and perpetuate the culture of an organization.[9] Organization culture is shaped and its character devised from a firm's unique historical roots, its situational development as it has responded to internal and external forces in its growth cycle. It reflects not only on employees but also relationship dealings with customers and suppliers as well as responses to competitors. Organizational culture tends to be forced acceptance as opposed to the more hidden reinforced acculturation occasioned by acquiring culture via birthright, the passive accumulation of geographical influences and the volunteered or sought after educational elements that all result in acquiring one's cultural acquisitions in the tiered building system per Figure 1.2.

The first two layers, birthright and geographical, of cultural development are the deepest felt, the most difficult to change, and vary the most as one moves from one society to another. The top two layers, educational and organizational, may by their broader indoctrination acquisition

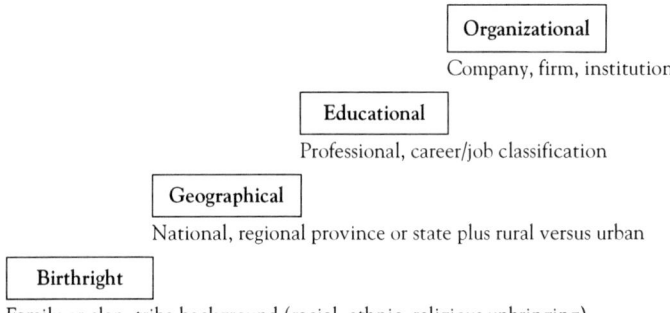

Figure 1.2. Cultural building staircase: levels of group induced affiliations.

surpass the constraints of the more limited originating family/geographical inputs thereby allowing for greater flexibility, alteration, and change. People are more apt to modify the higher educational institutions they attend much less than the subjects they major in and the collateral courses selected. The same occurs over their business careers they tend to adjust their professional associations and certainly move from company to company; a readjustment of organizational culture but continue to perform many of the identical tasks within them.

Examining One's Cultural Self-Identity

An exercise based on the various group affiliations one is exposed to in life, the levels of cultural indoctrination as provided by other associations to induced self-identity is proposed by Taylor Cox, Jr. and Ruby L. Beale in their book on managing diversity.[10] The activity, with the goal of increasing awareness of one's socially induced self-identity, directs one to create a "pie chart" based on two dimensions of diversity related to one's group affiliations in their lives by indicating the approximate importance of membership in groups as represented by the size of the slice of pie assigned to them. An evaluation of one's primary associations (e.g., sex and orientation, race, ethnicity, age, physical and mental abilities) and secondary associations (education, income, marital and parental status, religion, political affiliation, work experience as well as hobbies, grooming and clothing style, music preference) provide the criteria for assessment. This combination of forces, under the control or inducement of others, and self-selected group affiliations examines how people categorize themselves and hence allows for an insight into one's cultural profile as well as indicating the force or influence these associations exert on the individual. While the criteria are much wider than the four cultural levels concept that begins with the family and progresses up to organizations, it can be a valuable tool in assessing one's cultural drivers. The only drawback to the exercise is that the journey to self-discovery is complicated and a number of false positives may be encountered as the integration of associations tends to contaminate one another as opposed to direct linkages specifically affecting behavior and perceptual thinking. A simpler, less complex set of cultural components or determinants might afford a better guide to one's cultural self-identity.

The Cultural Pond

Another way to visualize the cultural development of the individual but with an added component is the undulating pebble in the pond example. As a small stone is dropped in the center of the water, a ripple upon which the individual cultural ship sails is created. The vessel containing one's cultural identity is propelled outward engaging larger and wider cultural experience and assimilation as the ship moves out through ever expanding circles (see Figure 1.3). It first passes through the family unit absorbing both the surface and deep undercurrent characteristics. As the pebble, birth cultural development, sinks at this spot in the pond it more

Figure 1.3. Cultural circles.

intensively draws down the cultural affinity, almost anchoring the ship. The cultural ship's journey moves through the three remaining circles encountering the geographical area then passing the educational segment and finally progressing across the organizational area.

The cultural pond is at its deepest at the center, the spot of initial contact of the pebble and the start of the ship's cultural journey. The water depth drops off as the bottom rises as one ventures out and collaterally so does the intensity of the influential conditioning the cultural pond provides. Think in terms of a right-angled triangle lying on its side with the family providing the strongest influence and in descending order geographical, educational, and organizational (see Figure 1.4).

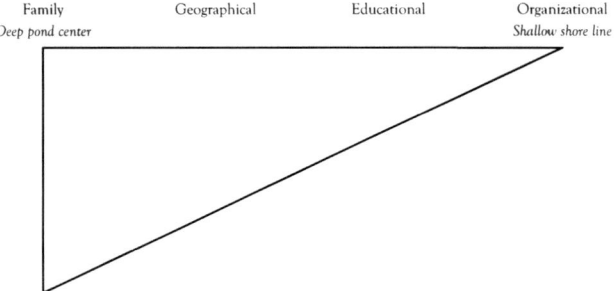

Figure 1.4. *Cultural pond depth: from deep to shallow influence.*

Cultural Push Back: *Culture Shock*

Calm sailing of the cultural ship normally occurs as one progresses outwardly and comes to rest on the eventual shoreline of their own pond. However as one crosses over the land bridge to a new culture the track can be torturous as one's cultural security is threatened. Sometimes the beach terrain is uneven and rocky or ends at an embankment such as natural cliffs or a man-made sea wall. The cultural wave that propelled in their home pond does not gently wash up and over to a new alien cultural pond. The waters upon which one's cultural ship ventures is repelled backwards and may be forced to recede. An upsurge in the surf occurs, disturbing the tranquility of the home or domestic cultural pond affecting one's emotional and rational mind-set. This push back is cultural shock. Cultural shock is theoretically defined as the "psychological reaction to an unfamiliar or alien environment" referred to by Kalervo Oberg as "a generalized trauma one experiences in a new and different culture because of having to learn and cope with a vast array of new cultural cues and expectations, while discovering that your old ones probably do not fit or work."[11]

The more different the shoreline obstruction erected by the alien society is from one's domestic waters the stronger the reverse wave and the cultural ship is tossed around, upsetting the navigational balance and affecting its structural identity. Americans traveling to their northern neighbor Canada would experience minimal culture shock as the two countries share an abundance of similarities making up the radiating circles; and one might be said to be sailing on a conjoined cultural pond feed from related cultural springs. As one "jumps across the pond," a common vernacular expression for crossing the Atlantic Ocean to Europe, a stop in England, a nation that shares a common heritage and basic language with the United States (accent and terminology aside), might not be so shocking but certainly more then a Canadian venture. Moving east onto Europe increased cultural strains might be encountered. As one ventures south and further east, across the Mediterranean onto the African continent, the Middle East and still further east toward the Asian subcontinent and into China the divide between East and West, first mentioned in the Introduction, gets wider and the push back or cultural shock deepens, becoming more acutely felt on all the senses. While initially the disturbing feeling occasioned by entering culturally alien societies tends to be on the surface of the cultural iceberg (see Figure 1.1) the physical observed differences, those below the surface, mind-sets affecting core values and therefore determining beliefs, attitudes, outlooks, and perceptional realities begin to rise, psychologically affecting the cross-cultural engager. One has a natural tendency to retreat to what they feel is normal, deeply desirous of the safety of their ingrained learned cultural attitudes and beliefs, their pond, as they attempt to combat alien cultures.

The push back can be just a mere ripple or a more destructive intensive undulation akin to a rip tide. It is felt most dramatically in descending reverse order as it moves offshore to deeper home cultural waters. Organizational or institutional culture is first affected as it based in shallower waters. Then to a lesser but still strong degree educational culture, then to a minor extent geographical and finally to the least amount family culture as this element is most deeply entrenched in higher waters, anchored in the middle of the pond. Within a business context one may first notice differences in institutional hierarchy structuring, the organizational circle, duties, responsibilities, and decision-making roles; the way things get done within a group vary. Strategic goals may be based on alternative value assessments. Time orientations and meeting models may differ. Parties that share professional backgrounds, the educational circle, with similar sounding titles or positions are not equal in how they apply basic skill sets and interact with other segments of the company. The regulatory and economic environment the alien business operates in, the geographical circle, impacts operational activities. The infrastructure, from communication in marketing programs to affected channels of trade and distribution, may differ. Commercial relationships whose underpinnings stem from one's personal indoctrinations, the family circle, may not be established in the same way. Individual versus collective group objectives are not uniform with one cultural determinant taking precedence over the other.

The process of acculturation, a hopefully gentle immersion into a new society, is not easy and recognizing this is important. It is this backdrop of cultural development, its acquisition and potential disruption, that international managers must first appreciate and understand before their formal education on the subject begins. A cross-cultural education enables one to build a *bridge over troubled water*[12] allowing our individual ships to sail smoothly between one's home harbor ponds and those inhabited by alien societies while minimizing culture shock.

Other Aspects of Culture

Culture as Acquired Knowledge

Culture is a process wherein one acquires the knowledge to deal with accepted social behaviors in a given group or society. The process is characterized by a series of key factors. It is a learning experience (a) passed on from one generation to the next, (b) mutually shared with others resulting in common outlooks and responses of a group, (c) exemplified by interlocking cross-influential patterns that sustain and play off each other, (d) observable via commonly understood symbols and finally part of a (e) fluid state with adaptive changes altering all of the previous contributing factors.

Culture as a Sensory Filter

Culture is the prime motivator of our conscious and unconscious thought. It influences our brain and heart, impacts our rational determinations and emotional intuitions. It is the filter of our senses, what we see, hear, smell, taste, and touch. The inputs from these collectors are interpreted, assigned values and therefore classified as important or not, depending upon our cultural indoctrinations. Culture determines our value system and prejudices our perceptions. While we all see the same things, like peering through the lens of a camera, the imprint process on the film of our brain causes different culturally induced images to appear. The colors and the shades are altered. Some images are sharp while others are grainy or out of focus. The expression "don't you see it" is most appropriate as in fact we don't all see identically. The axiom "beauty is in the eyes of the beholder" is true and exemplifies our cultural induced bias as we unconsciously apply our predetermined socially induced beliefs, values and traditions dispositions.

The Ethnocentric Nature of Culture

One of the dangers of culture is that it creates and supports ethnocentric dispositions. It is natural for one to think that their way is the best or correct way and such presumptive thinking is an impediment to being open to the acceptance of alien cultures. Ferraro defines ethnocentrism as "literally 'culture centered'—the tendency for people to evaluate a foreigner's behavior by the standards of their own culture and believe that their culture is superior to all others."[13] When confronted by difference, instead of re-evaluating our own stance on issues there is a penchant to fail back on what one has first learned and treat such knowledge as sacrosanct; failing to recognize our own biases. This is the trapdoor in the cultural learning process and one must be ever vigilant not to fall through it.

Cultural Stereotyping

We all come equipped with a nuanced picture of the world called cultural stereotyping. It is the product of retained memory and learned patterns of associations. Such dual programming often results in snap judgments about those we meet with preconceptions of expectations. While cultural investigating and the process of providing value determinants to access and qualify the pronounced group characteristics of particular societies is a valuable guidance tool in both understanding and appreciating social interaction and relationship development, it has its dangers. There is a marked tendency to prejudge relative similarities or differences between two cultures based on applied research and quantified historical inspectional criteria. To stereotype people and place them into prelabeled categories so one can know what to expect and hence plan to act and react accordingly seems to be a reasonable and prudent device. It is a very natural consideration, like doing one's homework in advance and being prepared; an axiom we have all heard. In doing so there is a related risk, as all too often caricature-based descriptions of people can contain oversimplifications, biased images and impressions, gossip, and myth related stories resulting in a clichéd profile of a society. Best to resist this temptation and therefore tread lightly between the factual and the fictional.

What the study of culture and the principles used in the examination process should really be intended for is to provide a template for investigation as opposed to generating predisposed dispositions of expected values, behavior, and attitudes. A knowledge of culture is best applied when it is joined by observation and experience. One's cultural education is best used when it allows for the actual input to be correlated with definitive criteria and a meaningful classification system. In other words create a reservoir of information that allows one to be a cultural detective. Besides first appreciating one's own cultural profile, watch, monitor, and examine others before forming cultural opinions, then correlate such familiarity into usable understandable and workable knowledge on how to best engage and form relationships with new parties.

The RDF Syndrome

Egocentrism and stereotyping can result in the creation of a reality distortion field (RDF), a delusional alteration of reality created by one's own mind-set as alien environments are encountered.[14] The concept refers to a blinded state of mind when one's normal sensory faculties are hampered by preset cultural orientations preventing one from perceiving reality and substituting fictional interpretations. It is a conditional result of applied egocentrism and preconceived stereotyping. The ingrained prejudicial rhythms of perception cause one to interpret their surroundings by substituting an alternative reality for factual observations. As such, RDF not only causes a misinterpretation of the behaviors of others but can also affect cross-cultural education as it stymies one's ability to fully comprehend and appreciate how differences emerge as we continue to fall back on what we know and value, often dismissing an unusual approach because it does not correlate with our prior indoctrinations. There is a natural induced tendency that can prohibit a functioning open mind to acknowledge, much less accept actual differences. The RDF syndrome needs to be recognized as it is a hidden phantom guarding our mind-sets and our perceptional realities of others around us.

Cross-Cultural Education Reluctance

The coupling of egocentrism and stereotyping, both normative reactions in themselves, hamper the study of culture itself. Many students and trainees being given a cross-cultural indoctrination approach the matter with an uninterested or negative self-induced mind-set. They tend to ask "why don't they just be like us as surely our way of life is the best?" Or "I already know them and their outlooks are wrong." Others are just afraid. They feel threatened by being exposed to a different way of life feeling it may influence and therefore change them. Such natural affinities, the possible erosion of the self, one's cultural heritage, is a real concern. Those faced with differences often respond by proclaiming "just let me stick to what I know." This reaction is normal as the security they feel is placed in jeopardy and this bothers them. To question, much less alter one's prospective is also viewed as being unpatriotic to their national or ethnic background. To combat such natural affinities one needs to approach the subject just as a warrior prepares for battle or an athlete readies themselves for competition, getting to know your opponent as well as oneself. The process fortifies and sustains the cross-cultural combatant. Viewed in the parlance of strategic preparation, using a SWOT (Strengths, Weaknesses, Opportunities, and Threats) analysis, it is a most valuable tool. It can allow one to draw on their cultural potency, recognize their culturally induced limitations while seizing on culturally induced advantageous openings and combating coercion in their own cultural mind-sets and those of others. A cross-cultural education helps to enter into and solidify relationships. It does not destroy one's unique cultural identity, it just better prepares them for successfully venturing into alien societies. Notwithstanding the need to learn how to handle and work with different cultures in the era of globalization, managers know that diversity of opinion strengthens the strategic decision-making process, allows for ideas to be more fully vetted and in the end adds value. A cross-cultural indoctrination is the first step in learning how to harness this extra asset.

The Historical and Hence Transitional Nature of Culture

Robert N. Bellah, a respected American sociologist and educator, quite simply insisted that human beings shape culture that in turn shapes them reminding us that "We do not come from nowhere," that culture is embedded in history and as culture evolves "nothing is ever lost." The development of our cultural world and the great traditions it created are still ingrained in us, defining what we are today as well as in the future. Bellah points to the origin of culture as examined through the lens of religion in the civilizations that emerged in the axial age; ancient Israel, classical Greece, Confucian China, and Buddhist India.[15] Whatever historical period is used as a cultural lynchpin the important point is that an appreciation and an understanding of culture has a historic component. In his book *On China*, Henry Kissinger, reviewing the ups and downs of Sino-American relations, reaches into ancient Chinese history to define national characteristics noting that while differences in culture are apparent their chronological development provides the context in which to appreciate not just how but why they work.[16] According to Kissinger what separates the United States and China is not differences in political systems, democratic versus totalitarian, but culture and history. Therefore the key element to understanding the Chinese mind-set, the formation of impulses behind their behavior, or for that matter any societal mind-set, is an understanding of historical events that impacted their society starting with Confucianism in 449 BC. While he begins with four generational influential times intertwined with the people that inspired them, he ends up with six; and in fact his book seems to offer a trail into the modern era filled with incidents that altered the psychological and philosophical make-up of the Chinese mind-set, their culture.

No culture remains completely static and at intervening periods, it is and will always be subject to change; arguably at different rates and to varying degrees. Some conservative cultures deeply protective of their equilibrium will resist the forces of change but nevertheless change is a constant feature impacting culture. Cultural alteration occurs from both inside and outside mechanisms. The development of Confucianism, per the aforementioned Kissinger book, was an internal discovered invention that has influenced and guided Chinese culture for centuries thereafter. Change can also come about externally as a result of borrowing from other cultures, the process of acculturation. Historic events play an important part in cultural diffusion, the spreading of ideas from one culture to another. However, in the absence of war, the most proficient agent of change across and between cultures is trade.

The Cultural Mind-Set Often Stays Hidden

A key phrase in Arabic is *tahta tawila*, with versions of the phrase appearing in the languages of all Muslim countries in the Middle East while also found in South Asian dialects. While the literal translation is "under the table," colloquially it is used to describe the idea that nothing is as it appears; a good description for the covert or hidden aspects of culture. Whatever is stated or portrayed as proof is irrelevant and intended to conceal what goes on behind the scenes, a place out of sight where everything that is important is revealed. Real intent is therefore obscured or masked. Words, gestures, and body language often hide the true agenda of the parties. This concept was taught to me by my father although he was unfamiliar with the Arabic terminology. He advised me to always be cognizant of the underlying direction someone wants to take you in, that engaged dialog does not always reveal the hidden agendas people wish to pursue.

Only through the study of culture can the mind-set of others be uncovered and thereby understood and appreciated. The fact that others may talk like you, wear the same clothing, enjoy the same food is the false positive of cultural similarity. How one thinks and organizes their thoughts, what one values and hence what motivates them as well as their perceptual filter of life around them are all culturally induced. Cross-cultural knowledge is the key to unlocking the identity of others as well as ourselves. It is therefore the most important skill that global managers need to acquire.

A Universal Culture?

The study of cultural anthropology is based on the simple principle that although all societies face similar problems, how they react to and handle them is uniquely different. Universal needs exist and the solutions to them result in basic methodologies being employed throughout the world. People everywhere construct similar generic templates to handle life. From the basic unit, family life, to socioeconomic and political structures to educational and supernatural belief systems all cultures create such associations. Some aspects of these organizational models share similarities while others vary greatly.

Do all human beings possess common cultural characteristics that they value to the same or approximate degree? As we all share biological structural similarities and fundamental physiological natural needs, nourishment, shelter, safety and procreation drives, do any universal mind-sets emerge?

The idea of a universal shared culture approached from a strict scientific inspection, physical anthropology, which traces the development of humanoid (human like) species on earth, would seem to be a sustainable principle. Anthropological researchers have long maintained that man had his beginning on the African continent. Relying on the spread theory of mankind eventually dispersal across the globe followed. Proof of this generally accepted idea is that genetic analysis indicates that "there is a greater genetic variety among the inhabitants of Africa than anywhere else in the world. This is exactly what one would expect if human beings had originated there."[17] If all races and creeds around the globe have an identical anthropological DNA heritage due to a common basic source, it follows that we are all related to a degree, and must therefore share at least one or many universal mind-sets and hence behavioral resemblances.

It is upon such premises that the study of culture is based; the search for similarities. But as noted at the beginning of chapter 2 the definition of cultural anthropology also includes differences. It is the hijacking of this common denominator imperative side of the cultural equation and the accent on what separates us as opposed to what unifies us that most books and articles on cross-cultural indoctrinations are based on. If, however, we educate cross-cultural engagers to focus on what we all share instead of concentrating on our differences the apparent cross-cultural divide would be more easily spanned and bridges of commonality would be constructed.

To paraphrase John Dunne, no man is an island unto himself and we do require others to live or simply to survive. Such a Darwinian approach would seem to imply that mankind has an innate need to balance individualism with collectivism, to achieve one's personal/private life sustaining needs by engaging in the establishment of relationships with others to provide for his own welfare. Mankind shares this instinctive motivational drive with all species on earth. "David Sloan Wilson, an evolutionary theorist at the State University of New York at Binghamton, sees the onset of humanity's cooperative, fair-and-square spirit as one of the major transitions in the history of life on earth, moments when individual organisms or selection units band together and stake their future fitness on each other."[18] Although Wilson's statement is housed in the developmental evolution of mankind all life on earth evolved when a large bacterial cell engulfed a smaller one to form the first complex eukaryotic cell and this fundamental process was followed by uniquely designed single cells merging into multicellular organisms of specialized parts. At the core of this scientific inspection is the study of the symbiotic relationship between an individual and the union with others, a collective drive. Common plants grow in similar terrains and climate environments from forests to grasslands while even under water they grow in ocean fields together. Insects group in colonies and hives. Fish swim in schools while ocean mammals are found in packs. Some animals move in herds while others hunt and raise their young in prides. The willingness of all things on earth to work cooperatively is a universal imperative. All species form unions of their own kind but this natural feature or bio-socio template does not result in a completely egalitarian system and the demise of the individual. Gradients of individualism and the rate or degree to which one is absorbed into the collective system are exhibited by all life. In human form different societies strike varying balances between the individual and group associations and such relationships remain at the core of characteristics of all things. While all of life's living creatures store and share the necessities of life no other species on earth, except humans, participates in the exchange process, one thing for another. The idea of trade, culminating in a commercial system, is one of the primary examples of the individual engaging in a social interaction—a group function. Gerard Delanty argues that the most appropriate way of theorizing cultural diversity is to situate it in the context of a broad rational theory of culture in which the key dynamic is cultural encounters.[19] Modern globalization is perhaps the largest world stage upon which social actors engage each other on a constant 24/7 basis. An examination utilizing this process is therefore a valuable template upon which to investigate cross-cultural matters.

CHAPTER 2

Culture and the Commercial Interloper

Culture can be examined on a commercial plane.
The trading initiative, a practice common to all societies, has been
and will continue to be an initiator of cultural change. It is therefore
an appropriate canvas upon which to examine and qualify cultural
considerations.

The behavioral science called the economics of societies has been, and remains today, a valuable asset in the pursuit of commercial success. The adaptability of the research and theoretical applications emanating from the study of cultural anthropology and the broader inspection of sociology has always contributed to the business imperative. Besides survival in its offensive or defensive mode and organizational spirit worship or religion to explain the unknown, economics, and at its root the process of exchange, is a prime contributor to the furthering of social interaction and cooperation. Trade is one of the major engines driving engagement with the environment as mankind has always used natural resources to develop and progress.

The desire to exchange is ingrained in the human existence. While all creatures on earth forge, hunt, and hoard or store, mankind is the only species on earth to practice this unique human trait. Trade is a universal activity and is to be found in all societies. It is one of the fundamental activities that all cultural groups engage in and hence it is a common denominator acting as a natural binding agent between them.

Laurence Bergreen, writing on the travels of Marco Polo, comments on the support offered by history's most self-chronicled explorer encountering alien societies in respect to similarities and not differences. In a telling observation of the practice of trade by people in foreign lands he relates that Polo concluded that such people must be civilized and not barbaric—perhaps exhibiting traits like us. As told by Bergreen, Polo is said to exclaim that "they are great merchants, ... and do great trade." With this endorsement, "he implies that first impressions notwithstanding, the inhabitants are fully human; to his way of thinking (Polo's), trading virtually defines their humanity."[1] It was on the rails of trade that the exchange of ideas, inventions, philosophical and religious thoughts moved from one region to another. Anthropologists tend to "generally agree that as much as 90% of all things, ideas and behavioral patterns found in any culture had their origins elsewhere."[2] The process of trade was a prime conduit for such cross-territorial cultural diffusion into other societies.

Early merchants were the first cross-cultural ambassadors. In antiquity the process of exchange or initially barter was based on interpersonal relationships. An understanding of the other party in such primitive transactions, what they needed, and what they valued, was dependent on appreciating how they lived. Bargaining material trade objects was early recognized as conditional on the mind-sets of the parties involved; in essence their culture as manifested in things and the value they placed upon them. As the trade initiative moved across and between clans and tribes people began to encounter differences which impacted the exchange process. With the eventual growth of the commercial endeavor across territories and on to intercontinental trade routes the need to be acquainted with the motivations of alien groups only grew in importance. As recounted in *Cathay and the World Thither*, a series of essays on the intercourse (trading ventures) between China and the Western nations in 1866, the need of merchants to familiarize themselves with the culture of the inhabitants of the alien territories encountered in their commercial journeys was paramount to the success of their activities.[3] Francis Balducci Pegolotti authored a guide on the commercial navigation of dealings on the famed Silk Road connecting East and West. Unlike the immensely popular semibiographical account of the journeys of Marco Polo over the same trade route and his time in the court of Kubla Khan, the great Chinese emperor, the Pegolotti treatise is a true cross-territorial guide with detailed information on the need for a deep appreciation and understanding of the customs, traditions, and ways—the culture—of the different social groups one will encounter and have to deal with for a successful series of bartered exchanges.[4]

The linkage between the cultural background of a given society and economic development of that group has been explored in countless books, journal articles, and essays. Most literature concludes that different cultures are reflective of basic socioeconomic and political systems around the world.[5] Hence commercial managers conducting business in varying environments, both regional and national, would be wise to consider the cultural influence on their widespread global development both at the strategic planning stage as well as everyday operational activities with all stakeholders—employees, suppliers, consumers, and the local community, as well as government authorities.

Economic Activity and Preservation of the Social Order

The Greek philosophers routinely commented in their dialogs on the relationships of people to each other and the world around them, in order to instruct one in the art of citizen skill that would lead to statecraft or statesmanship for the benefit of society. They referred to this as *politike*, a combination of the word *polites*, meaning citizen and the suffix *-ike*, denoting skillful application.

Within this context the modern word economics is attributable to the ancient activities of Greek society. The Greek word referring to one's habitat, essentially their household or family estate, is *oikos* from which the prefix "eco" is derived. The Greek word denoting the management of or careful stewardship over one's property is *nomos*. When combined they formed the basis for a thesis by the Greek author Xenophon called *Oikonomia or Oeconomica*, which roughly translated means "Household Management," a guide to handling the affairs of one's estate. A concept noted in chapter 1 by Sedlacek relates economics as a social science, the art of helmsmanship.

Interestingly, while many scholarly offerings on the origin of the term economics attribute it to Aristotle, he "wrote on practically anything under the sun, but what he conspicuously did not write on was economics."[6] One of the steps in acquiring *politike* was the study of *oikonomia* or economics as such skills could be duplicated to a degree in properly organizing the affairs of the state; that is, the wise and prudent maintenance of a city-state's physical surroundings by orchestrating a combination of human labor and natural resources to produce beneficial results. Simply stated, if one could master the running of an estate such lessons would be helpful in managing the socio-political environment. Therefore the economics of Aristotle, as well as his predecessors Socrates and Plato that influenced him, does not correspond nor relate to the modern day term economy. Aristotle did however refer to this term as a human science in his commentaries on the public management of state affairs and how Greeks, meaning the aristocratic landed gentry, should best organize their lives around the common good or as he saw it, the welfare of the state.[7] Early Greek philosophers tended to view the process of exchange or barter as a behavior based on proportional reciprocity, a tacit reference to virtue or ethics in dealing with others. They viewed the process as a necessary component to the normal establishment of social relationships. *Oikonomike* (economics) was the Greek adjective Aristotle used to refer to activities related to the use of wealth in order to achieve the good and just life.[8]

Within this limited context they did not understand nor appreciate that such numerous individual transactions to sustain and promote human relationships could result in a separate and distinct system of commercial activity unto itself. The idea of a profit incentive immersed in the exchange of physical things, creating a free market pricing for products never was part of their thinking. They duel fully recognized that trade played an essential part in sustaining social development, and therefore concluded that the state should be involved in economics. They did not see the commercial system as a separate condition but as a mere extension of human interaction, the prime subject that they devoted their writings and lectures to. They tended to philosophize the commercial experience investigating motives behind the process. They saw it as illustrative of behavioral relationships, concentrating on the values attached to it, almost approaching the subject as a cultural anthropology examination. In essence they examined the dichotomy between the individual and the collective activities of society they needed to interact with. The social commentary of the ancient Greek philosophers and the themes of the authors of poems and plays of the day used the field of economics as a societal window to view human behavior, attitudes, beliefs, and values; the fundamental aspects of cultural manifestation.

Referencing the work of Moses Finley in his 1973 book *The Ancient Economy* more recent authors Sheidel and Von Reden describe ancient economic activity as a socially inspired mechanism as opposed to a separate sphere from social relations and political matters. They cite the Finley proposition stating "that considerations of status and civil ideology, rather than the laws of supply and demand, governed economic decision making." Further that economics in the Greco-Roman world was intertwined with intrapersonal associations and the activities surrounding it "were embedded in a network of social relationships that determined values, attitudes and actual behaviour."[9] From estate management by the elite landed gentry to the labors in the fields by peasant-citizens to ensure their family's subsistence, the incentives for profit seeking behavior are seen as political (public relationships) rather than economic in nature.[10]

An inspection into the idea of economics as a social instrument was introduced in the East in the Indian treatise *Arthasastra* by Kautilya. This massive series of essays to guide secular social behavior did not emerge from a religious inspiration nor was it proclaimed in a specific codex of laws. The 15 books comprising the writings were intended as a strategic blueprint for rulers of a domain—a set of policy instructions. Scholars have attempted to translate the world "arthasastra" in order to better define and explain its extensive commentary to achieve an ordered civilization. As such it has been referred to as the "science of politics… material use of or science of wealth…political economy"[11] mimicking to a degree the same approach the Greek philosophers used in incorporating *oikonomike* into their works to accomplish the same end. In academic and business circles it is synonymous with economics, with Kautilya considered the first management guru. Kautilya believed that a resilient and progressive society is built on sound economic policy. The *Arthasastra*, although not a legal code, sets down principles of required behavior of a nation's citizens and as such reads like a blueprint for cultural expectations in a given group. In *Book IV, The Removal of Thorns*, a number of chapters are devoted to the treatment and obligations or culturally engineered responses and behaviors of those involved in commercial trade. One chapter discusses artisans, another focuses on merchants. *Book III* in the collection has a chapter on the use of common laborers and slaves.[12] Although not considered a cultural anthropological inspectional tool, the *Arthasastra* text uses the process of exchange or trade as the platform on which to construct cultural determinants and their effect on a society.

Guang Zhong, a Chinese philosopher, in his book *Guan Zi,* mixed the philosophical motivations of individuals, their standards, attitudes, and behaviors as exemplified in their particular culture, in the context of societal economics. He felt that one's quest for profit, which he described as personal material gain or wealth accumulation, would drive one to make right choices in life without the intervention by administrative government directed policies based on the collective good. He again used economics, as did the Greek and Indian theorists, as the inspection vehicle to examine and comment on culturally induced decision making value determinants. Chuang Tzu, following the philosophy of Lao Tzu, one of the central figures in Taoism, proclaimed that individuals should be left to their pursuit of contentment as driven by their cultural indoctrinations and that "good order (in a society) results spontaneously when things are left alone."[13] The Chinese historian Sima Qian, in essays written around 206 BC, describes a natural order of man to maximize self-interest within a value induced orderliness of exchange without guided interference, a market system he calls *the way.* The idea has been likened to the invisible hand mechanism later made famous by Adam Smith in *The Wealth of Nations.*[14] The reference to self-interest recognizes that man should be left to his own abilities and exert his own strengths to obtain what he wishes, but often motivated by a shared communal value, beliefs, attitudes, and behavior; in essence his cultural indoctrination. In the Middle and Near East region business was and is today greatly influenced by the Islamic religious faith, as all activities in life, as determined by one's cultural mind-set, are practiced with a strong reverence to its teachings. Abu Hamid Al-Ghazal, a theologian of Sunni thought and philosopher offers a commentary on the role of economics in society. He states that: "Man's inability to fulfill all his needs alone persuades him to live in a civilized society with cooperation: but tendencies like jealousy, greed, competition and selfishness, can create conflict. Therefore, some collective arrangement becomes necessary to check those tendencies."[15] The repeated reference to the word "tendencies," as well as the descriptive words that follow illustrating the term, are indicative of culturally induced behavior in forming relationships with others within the framework of a system—the "collective arrangement," or market formed by individual transactions. Al-Ghazal considers a free marketplace to be one in which mutual needs of a buyer and seller are satisfied via their shared or common values; in essence asking each party to recognize and respect as well as be guided by the culturally induced mind-sets of the other which produces an ethical result in the exchange transaction. He links culture to business as a valued mechanism to achieve equitable respect.

What all of the aforementioned ancient writers seem to agree on is that economics and its chief agent, the commercial imperative, provide for an excellent host environment in which to study mankind's relationship with others—cultural anthropology. The goal of people and the institutions they create to pursue commercial ventures has at its measurable core a striving for, and accumulation of wealth, with the prime quantifiable criteria money and/or property, both tangible (physical or real) and intangible (proprietary rights) that have a corresponding monetary value. Philosophically scholars have demonstrated that money and its representative equivalents "operated as a signifier by which relationships, identity and power" …even "sovereignty, religious authority and justice" could be exercised.[16] In essence, the commercial arena is a great exemplifier of mankind's attitudes and beliefs, their values, and behaviors; and as such makes for an excellent medium in which to research and inspect cultural anthropology and construct meaningful guidelines for understanding its contextual makeup. The works of these authors also underscore the development of culture within the framework of the balancing of personal needs with the society around them. This tells us that at the core of one's mind-set identity is the relationship between the person and their group. This dichotomy is described and referred to in cultural determinant language as individualism versus collectivism.

Economic Systems and the Cultural Factor

The proposal that one of the cultural determinants, individualism versus collectivism, is the prime component to guide one through the cross-cultural melee that managers must contend with is echoed in other discussions on economic thought. As previously noted, early philosophers from every culture in the world based their inspection of the social order, a cultural profile, on the blending or balancing of individual interests with the collective needs of the society around them. In a more modern context the debate pitting laissez-faire capitalism against governmental intervention in commercial affairs, the business of people and their relationships, is the subject of a book by Wapshott, *Keynes-Hayek: The Clash That Defined Modern Economics*. Nancy Koehn, offering a review of the book[17] reflects on the arguments of these two intellectuals by asking two questions to characterize their relative positions on the make-up of society; "How much faith do we have in individual agency? And what do we owe to our fellow citizens and our collective future?" The dichotomy between individualism and collectivism is again used as the prime inspection tool to understand and appreciate differences between societies; albeit on a economic level but certainly reflective of the wider inquiry into navigating the cross-cultural world. Mankind satisfies its personal primeval needs in life on three levels. Emotionally via family and friends, spiritually via a religious and/or philosophical affiliation and materially through the exchange or trade process. How we determine our behavioral actions based on such mind-set value criteria is in essence our cultural signature; and individualism intertwined with collectivism is the key dimension. Cohen's article *Don't disregard the importance of defining culture* reminds us that even in the face of military destruction following the Second World War two devastated countries, Germany and Japan, stripped of infrastructure and resources, again rose to economic prominence. His point is based on a Financial Times page one announcement that Volkswagen and Toyota are today's two world leaders in the automotive industry. However Cohen states "But it wasn't about cars. It was about culture—the most important story of our times." His explanation is their cultural heritage, as after the devastation that was all they "were left with." While professing that he cannot define the term culture he describes it as "something within us individually and something collectively within a nation or people."[18] The use of individualism and collectivism as the prime instruments comprising culture is most telling as even a novice writer in the field of social anthropology recognizes this determinant as mankind's paramount stimulator for dealing with life's accomplishments.

Religion and Globalization, the Cultural Component

Two articles placed on the Web the same day deal with a religious approach to the economic, financial, and moral crises arising out of globalization. The first was on a proposal for reforming the global financial system released by the Vatican on October 24, 2011. Contained in the document is the reported comment of Pope Benedict XVI that "it is not possible … to pursue the common good while also glorifying the values of utilitarianism and individualism."[19] By the term "common good" the Pope is referring to a collective motivation that is in opposition to private interest or as he states "individualism." In essence he is describing the prime cultural determinant that controls our values and behavior—the integration of individualism versus collectivism.

The second article was an interview with Chief Rabbi Jonathan Sacks of the United Hebrew Congregations of the Commonwealth (United Kingdom).[20] Also commenting on the effect of globalization he states "We pass our genes on as individuals but we survive in groups…So we are caught in the perennial tension between the drive to good, and instinct to self-preservation that sees everyone as a means to our ends." The Rabbi is again depicting the interwoven dichotomy between "good" by which he means, as the Pope states, the "common good," and the desire for personal fulfillment. Further along in the interview the Rabbi is quoted as posing the question: "How do we weigh that up in our minds?—what does our cultural induced mind-set tell us? At that crucial moment of decision, do I say it's 'me first', or, 'I have responsibilities to others who put their trust in me'?" Just like the Pope this religious leader frames human values in terms of a balance between individualism and collectivism.

Both these learned men striving to give direction to their followers on how to properly respond to life's issues reach an identical conclusion.

The key to "everything that people have, think and do,"[21] their cultural affinity, is contained in the prime cultural determinant individualism versus collectivism, and this dimension drives all the others.

Modern Drivers of Globalization

While the principles of globalization were planted in the cross-territorial activities of antiquated merchants the wider scope and greater degree of today's internationally linked economies demands that global managers must master cross-cultural skills. The population of the world is projected to grow from its present 7 billion, a level reached in November 2011, to 9.2 billion by 2050. What were once labeled as developing or emerging nations, exemplified by such countries as South Korea, China, India, and Brazil, are today moving toward an economic status to rival the 1960s' dominating triad of the United States, Western Europe, and Japan. The world is technologically shrinking into a more manageable marketplace with more players—suppliers, producers, and customers. As multinational companies expand their activities around the world to adjust to the new global environment there is an increased need to be operationally and administratively efficient across and between differing national societies. A review of the drivers of modern globalization well illustrates the pressing need to be favorably versed in understanding and appreciating one's own culturally induced mind-set as well as those of alien cultures that need to be engaged in the exchange process.

Market Drivers

Sales expansion into new markets as well as to gain economies of scale drive globalization. As the world has grown more and more consumers have begun to have similar needs and wants. This phenomenon has resulted in the emergence of universal uniform global consumerism. It is coupled with and driven by similar influential marketing methods to persuade them as well as more and more common venues or platforms of distribution channels shared around the world. In spite of such pronounced movement to serving customers on a parallel or analogous basic platform multinational companies have recognized that they must learn to tweak, alter, or modify their product's physical characteristics, trademarks, pack size, and graphics as well as the advertising inducement messages to reach varying values, attitudes, and the overall motivational purchase decisions that are culturally still different around the world. Even the physical layouts of global retail chains' establishments as well as Internet shopping websites need to address culturally induced variations.

It follows that, "If you want to sell globally, you have to source globally"[22] and the next driver naturally emerges.

Resource Drivers

Initially commercial entities going abroad did so for material resource attainment from new territories, with the second motivator further driven by the search for low cost labor production. On the heels of these historic drivers modern firms have begun to look for pockets of knowledge and innovation to augment their domestic home base research and development activities (R&D). Such increased involvement on a people-to-people basis, bringing ideas together as opposed to physically separated raw materials and the fruits of geographically separated labor sources, requires a deeper and more extensive implementation of cross-cultural indoctrinations. Understanding how people think and form relationships with others is the key to achieving successful cooperative R&D worldwide ventures as well as attaining wide global resourced materials and utilizing dispersed labor inputs.

Given the dual drivers, to place output and to acquire input, world competition is growing.

Competitive Drivers

Today, the reasons for foreign development have been augmented and expanded. Firms, to remain competitive in their respective industries, need to defend their home turf (domestic marketplace) from intruders by attacking the home bases of the commercial interlopers forcing such entities to defend their own markets from new competitors. More and more companies are looking for overseas alliances and joint ventures—to ally themselves with other firms to fend off global competitors. This pronounced initiative to form associations with foreign companies requires them to establish common strategic goals and cooperative tactics to achieve them. Such desire in turn necessitates that diverging cultural mind-sets must find similar patterns of thought upon which to build allied and valued relationships.

Beyond the prime global commercial players, sellers and buyers, and the associations formed between them the world stage also encompasses governments.

Governmental Drivers

Cumbersome and restrictive regulations of some nations, especially developed countries, with regard to environmental laws, labor codes, drug testing, and tax regulations to name just a few, have forced certain industries to look for more liberal areas to place their operations in. Add to this desire changes on the global political landscape to embrace forms of capitalism and the movement from state-owned industries to privatization has created another player in the globalization game—government. This important driver requires global managers to work with varying administrative hierarchical structures and personnel that are also influenced by national culturally based imperatives. All of these globalization drivers require a working knowledge of and the skillful application of cross-cultural techniques.

Technology, the Fuel of Globalization

While not a driver of globalization per se advancements in technology or IT have propelled the modern onslaught of the global commercial initiative fueling its accelerated growth and rapid expansion. While the mechanism of globalization has been constructed via the aforementioned fundamental commercial drivers the energy needed to take full advantage of them are the breakthroughs in new inventions and designs that have literally shrunk the world into a more manageable seamless network. The key component is increased communication between people even providing for the cost-efficient physical movement of goods.

The tools of network connection have resulted in a *hyper-connected flat world.*[23] Technical hardware, from the cell phone with all its apps and text messaging capabilities to fax machines along with Internet generated emails and teleconferencing that also provided the foundation for social networks like Facebook and Twitter have placed the world in an instantaneous 24/7 communication state. A seamless network of information allows not only for the real-time exchange of ideas and data, but the constant monitoring of container shipments to small package delivery of raw materials and components to factories and the onward distribution of finished products into the hands of consumers. Behind the proper successful use of such technological advancements is a cross-cultural underpinning as such devices are manned by people from various cultural backgrounds.

Measurable Effect of Cultural on International Business

Shankar in his 2011 award winning article regarding cultural distance (CD) offers a measurement criterion based on multiple areas of business activity across and between borders as motivated by the aforementioned drivers.[24] He shows how numerous international contexts from foreign direct investment (FDI) to headquarters-subsidiary relations to expatriate selection and adjustments are affected by the CD construct. He concludes that every aspect of a multinational corporation's (MNC) activities, from the strategic determination to go abroad to the selection of a market entry vehicle, to the actual running of operations within and without the organization has a CD element. And further that the performance success or failure of a MNC is not only traceable to but very dependent on cross-cultural conditions encountered. The preeminent factor and therefore a critical component for managers to master in today's globalization era is an appreciation of cross-cultural issues and the natural imperative that follows, gaining an educational understanding of how it influences international business.

The Global Commercial Wheelbarrow

The merger of globalization per the aforementioned drivers and the fuel of IT mechanisms act in unison like the two supporting balance rods that the modern global commercial wheelbarrow rests upon. But when the process is placed in motion, allowing for the forward repositioning of the wheelbarrow, the front steering wheel or cultural imperative needs to be engaged. For two balancing physical supports, the drivers and technology, to work successfully, effective cross-cultural communication must be installed.

Communication is the sending, encoding of messages, and receiving, decoding of messages by the brain. The process is laced with cultural relationship undertones. From the words chosen to the frequency and choice of medium used in the process the influential importance of cultural cannot be stressed enough. As Hofstede remarked, culture is the software of the mind and for the brain to function such input is required.[25]

Globalization and Culture

While the world is flattening, a colloquial description of globalization used by Friedman in his trilogy of books on the subject,[26] global managers are cautioned to *plan globally but react local, the global partnering dance.* This valuable guiding mantra recognizes the importance of cultural differences and their diverging effect on the tactical maneuvers used to achieve more universal strategic goals. While international business is driven by the aforementioned five global initiatives it is cultivated on cross-cultural relationships. The next chapter looks at the chronological development of cultural determinants constructed on the platform of global commercial dealings.

CHAPTER 3

Approaches to Cross-Cultural Understanding

Culture, First Pass—A Generic Overview

A number of generic oriented theoretical based classification headings are often cited to explain and characterize social behaviors of varying cultural groups. A concise review of them is a good way to initially examine the cross-cultural world. Presented as value comparisons they are:

- Approach to life—realistic pragmatic straightforward, no-nonsense versus idealistic philosophical with attention to past and present as worthwhile guides.
- Change acceptance—desired as it means improvement and necessary to attain growth in life versus accepted passively and not sought after as life should proceed at a steady rhythmic pace. Also proactive aggressive seeking of change versus flaccid reception of change to retain status quo.
- Competition worth—competition stimulates performance and results in better results versus competition can lead to disharmony and an unbalanced poorer result that does not satisfy the needs of all participants.
- Commitment honoring—doing what one says they will do and/or living up to a contractual agreement is sacrosanct versus mutual accords may be superseded or cancelled by conflicting emerging circumstances as they signify intention, not necessarily absolute adherence. (Note *force majeure* clause in legal instruments.)
- Initiative reward—hard work produces results and one can earn rewards quickly versus rewards may come to those after time as age determines one's role and status attainment

plus luck, preordainment, or the will of a supreme being is involved. Also best qualified succeed versus family, friendship, and other relationships determine success.

- Judgment appraisal—good and bad determination for any issue as things are seen either as reasonable or not, worthwhile or not versus determinations are relative and a middle ground incorporating both sides of an issue is desirable. Also what works, the end result/goal is paramount versus the process is equally and symbolically important as are results achieved.
- Teamwork accomplishment—working with others promotes more democratic or egalitarian values versus a strong authoritarian leader due to age, education, class, or lineage (family patriarch) may be in best position to guide a group
- Time use—to be idle is wasteful and unproductive (American adage "time is money") versus time is an unlimited resource to be enjoyed with schedules flexible.

Other Pertinent Nontheoretical Approaches

Aside from the theoretical research approach to cross-cultural inspection the globalization imperative has spawned literature devoted to the practical application of a required introduction for managers to operate more effectively in the international business field. As opposed to the technical collection of cultural determinants and their effect on global commercial relationships, an ideological introspection, more practical management guides on how to conduct one's overseas activities began to emerge in the mid-1980s. One of the earliest was *Going International* subtitled "How to Make Friends and Deal Effectively in the Global Marketplace."[1] This was one of the first books on culture I ever read and is still a valued reference. I have retained a copy in my personal library along with a very large host of textbooks accumulated during my managerial professional career and my academic tenure.

Instead of treating the subject from a cultural anthropology scientific position the book is introduced by examining the challenge of cross-cultural management from an American novice point of view, gently chastising U.S. businessmen as innocents abroad failing to meet the challenges of recognizing their own cultural characteristics while not taking the time and effort to understand and appreciate the varying and different traits of others. The authors go on to explain that getting the lie of the land crossing all business disciplines is paramount to fostering foreign entry success and sustaining positive results. As opposed to the concentration of most textbooks on managing cross-cultural relationships with employees, organizational cultural issues, as well as associations with external parties, suppliers, joint venture partners, and customers, the guidebook extends and relates the importance of cross-cultural knowledge to marketing—advertising and promotion—as well as the intricacies of cultural communication engineering in the social etiquette arena from greetings and orchestrating meetings to entertaining and gift giving. The stress on family entanglements for foreign travelers and expatriates from isolation to autonomy is also covered. The guide took research oriented cultural ideology and showed how it transected with the real world. Rules of cross-cultural engagement were constructed and further illustrated by anecdotes illustrative of the conceptual approaches the book provided. The book bridged the academic with the practical, and acted as my personal bible during my executive tenure. It pioneered the publication years later of popular titles like *Kiss, Bow or Shake Hands, How To Do Business in 60 Countries,*[2] and *Global Smarts, the art of communicating and deal making ANYWHERE in the world*[3] but the Copeland and Griggs book paved the way and made cultural education the new workable tool for the modern day global manager.

In 1979 Harris and Moran published *Managing Cultural Differences,* with the subtitle Leadership Strategies for a New World of Business.[4] The approach taken by these authors was to address cross-cultural indoctrination with leadership qualities that the new world of international business will require. It highlighted the attainment of effective performance by managers by utilizing cross-cultural skills across and between diversified groups. Instead of being organized around research oriented lists of cultural dimensions—only half a page is devoted to the widely referenced Hofstede model[5]—the book presents differences in managerial styles and approaches. It is essentially a training manual as opposed to a wide geographical tour guide with etiquette thrown in like the Bow books (although a section of the book is devoted to doing business with specific regional societies) or a deep scholarly research examination based on cultural anthropology platforms. The text even devotes pages to culture shock as introduced in chapter 2 and defined as the anxiety felt as one is acculturated into a new environment as well as the reverse syndrome when one returns to their home culture, reentry shock. During my own tenure as a global executive I experienced both phenomena. While I expected to a degree to feel the effects of culture shock in my travels, I did not realize that my foreign experiences would change me when I returned. Being exposed to numerous new cultural characteristics acted as a hidden transformation agent on my own mind-set. I vividly recall that during a social occasion with my good friends in my own home a few took me aside and asked what had happened to me. They explained that my outlook had changed, that I didn't seem to be like them anymore, and they were right. I simply saw the world from an enlarged perspective, questioning the indoctrinated values that I was brought up with. Over time I have been able to reconcile differences and better understand and appreciate the words of Socrates who said, "I am not an Athenian, I am not a Greek but a citizen of the World." The uniqueness of the Harris book is that it prepares one to combat cultural differences and adjust from a personal emotional perspective as opposed to covering the what to expect per functionary secular issues and the underlying academic inspection of why they occur. For me this valuable text has always been useful in my teaching duties to bridge the idealistic quasi scientific approach and the wider travel information guide. The cultural literary category amass with volumes offering wide generic managerial titles from the widely used *International Management: Managing Across Borders and Culture,*[6] to the lesser known *Global Comparative Management, A Functional Approach.*[7] A more limited perfunctory approach targeting the organization is exemplified by *International Dimensions of Organizational Behavior*[8] to *Managing Diversity, Toward a Globally Inclusive Workforce*[9] and *Global Management and Organizational Behavior.*[10] It should be noted however that many books on organizational or company culture are based on values, attitudes, and behaviors unique to that specific entity or institution as opposed to a cross-cultural context although an internal culturally diversified employee network contributes to the forming of such influential considerations.

These books are part of a massive array of featured titles containing the provocative words transcultural leadership and multicultural management. Many textbooks offering a wide introduction to the field of international business devote at least a chapter to cross-cultural issues while some weave a cultural component into other chapter sections. Add to such reference listings the vast amount of Internet sites devoted to cross-cultural information and the newly formed legends of consulting companies offering national seminars, on site, company customized programs as well as their own booklets and the subject is inundated by available materials. Even large multinational firms are offering their own training regimens conducted by internal cross-cultural human resource specialists. These activities are part of predeployment positioning for expatriate employees or for those that may have to interact on a part-time basis with their overseas operations accompanied by their own printed manuals, simulations, and immersion exercises.

Simply put, the field of cross-cultural indoctrination spans a wide parameter of applications for its use which it approaches from a wide variety of pedagogical disciplines. These inspections range from idealistic theory based underlying research oriented sets of determinants or dimensions, to secular real world how to conduct oneself guides like the Bow book, and on to leadership style training orientations, such as the Harris textbook. One enters a complicated world in pursuit of a cultural education. However, the process may be simplified if one breaks down the dense maze-like structure and erects a more direct approach. We will begin with a dissection of the theoretical, aim to find a core cultural factoring upon which all others are based, and use this prime element to graft on real-world applications and construct useful leadership tools.

Cultural Indoctrination, The New Prime Managerial Skill

The massive amount of research, a portion of which is addressed in this chapter, into the cultural aspects of business has prompted a new term to be coined. Researchers Christopher Earley and Soon Ang first presented the term *cultural intelligence* (CQ); defining it as an individual's capacity to adapt effectively in a cross-cultural environment or the globalized world.[11] Complementing an array of theories on the development and use of human intelligence, the idea of CQ both expands and codifies the importance of culture as a managerial tool, especially in the modern era of globalization as related in the following.

Introduction to Research Developed Cultural Determinants

Outside generalized theoretical references explaining the elements of culture the first inspection into human behavior was conducted within the framework of scholarly inquiry. The first widely published work began with Florence Kluckhohn and associates at Harvard University in the 1950s. The mythology applied consisted of a set of questions through which societies would find answers to the problems of everyday life.[12]

They were grouped as follows:

Human nature orientation—*are people seen as good* or *bad?*
Mankind's orientation to nature, the nonsocial human environment around them—*are people subjugated to, in harmony with, or maintain a desire to master the natural elements?*
Temporal orientation—*are people's time prospects directed to the past, present,* or *future?*
Activity orientation—*are people valued by their accomplishments/ achieving results (doing society)* or *their innate ascription or inherited personal traits (being society)?*
Relational orientation—*are people's relationships toward each other oriented to serving the specific needs of the individual* or *are one's commitments and obligations to a wider group for the collective good?*

The answers to the proposed questions set up definitive one way or the other rigid determination classifications using the word "*or*" (underlined in the above list) with little regard for the degree to which people prescribed to the alterative declarations. This classification system failed to recognize that a society might harbor elements of both sides of the separated spectrum embedded in their cultural make-up.

In 1975 John Condon and Fathi Yousef, in an examination of intercultural communications, expanded the five Kluckhohn question areas and proposed an additional 20 value dimensional inquiries.[13] They included factors correlated to:

- Gender dominance—*equality of the sexes as opposed to male hierarchy*
- Dispersal of authority—*democratic (egalitarian) society as opposed to an authoritarian (power held by few) political system*
- Social mobility—*either high or low*
- Social formality—*either high or low respect shown to others.*

At this stage of the research into and the development of cultural evaluation criteria there was a shift in the pedagogy from the Kluckhohn series of questions to a more specific dichotomy of inspectional terms with the use of the words "***opposed*** and ***or***" inserted. This creation of distinct separate points of reference—polar positioning extremes—was the forerunner for the methodology employed by researchers that followed. It did not, however, allow for societies to exhibit hidden or lesser facets of the alternating pillars, the duality factor, as only the dominant attributes were prescribed as indicative of a specific culture. With the added criteria "***high or low***" a more definitive designation was offered but no quantitative degrees were introduced so a breakeven point of difference to arrive at a high or low classification was difficult to establish. While this research contributed to the building of cross-cultural understanding it failed to present a complete measurable insight into all aspects of these influential determinants.

Hofstede's Dimensions

Gerte Hofstede was employed in the human resources department of the European headquarters of IBM. He was asked to develop a set of cultural inspectional tools to allow his employer, the multinational IBM company, to profile their far-flung international subsidiary managerial personnel.[14] The intention was to provide a template of mutual understanding that widely disbursed embedded managers around the world along with home office headquarters staff could utilize to better their cross-cultural relationships and provide for more uniform implementation of strategic plans and corporate policies. In essence, a universal platform to exchange ideas across and between a seamless managerial network without the interference of the cultural intrigue factor. He interviewed embedded managers of the company from around the world. From 1967 through 1973 the collected data from surveying over 100,000 employees in 49 different countries allowed him to analyze ways in which varying culturally induced mind-sets affected their on the job work related values, attitudes, and behaviors. He classified and cataloged his findings into four basic value determinate categories known as "Hofstede's Dimensions." Published in books and articles in the 1980s and 1990s they have become the most widely used paradigms in cross-cultural psychology having a profound influence on the field and practice of international business. They are used in undergraduate and graduate courses while chiefly presented in managerial seminars forming the underlying basis for the emergence of global consulting companies as well as culturally induced academic and commercial websites. As anthropology tools his set of determinants have been used to explain differences between cultural groups thereby promoting a better understanding of how they might work together to achieve common commercial goals.

The Hofstede collection comprised:

- Individualism *versus* collectivism/the interplay of people pursuing their own individual needs as opposed to working with and contributing toward group goals.
- Power distance—*high or low*/the acceptance of variances in social positioning as occasioned by those having command over others. A degree of preference for egalitarian versus hierarchical recognition and acceptance.
- Masculine *versus* feminine/a multifacet dimension wherein a society values material achievement, assertiveness, and competition as opposed to emotional nurturing, social relationship building, and cooperation. Task oriented versus relationship oriented. Also referred to as tough (masculine) versus tender (feminine) societies with conventional traditional separate roles for men and women.
- Uncertainty avoidance—*high or low*/degree of tolerance for risk taking with acceptance of ambiguity and unpredictability as opposed to a greater need for a more structured regulated life as people are risk intolerant and afraid of the circumstances attached to failure.

ADDED LATER—

- Long-term *versus* short-term orientation/the extent to which people are focused on the present (short-term) versus those taking an extended view into the future (long-term).
  The long-term orientation definition has also been extended backwards to include an appreciation of the past.

The Hofstede dichotomies continued the practice of categorizing cultures based on alternative propositions within the context of a singular cultural determinant with the use of the term, "*versus.*" He did however introduce a relative positioning by designating some determinants as "*high or low*," a semidegree factor as opposed to alternatives.

Country Clustering

In 1985, after conducting an integrative analysis of the available findings to date on cross-cultural determinants over 15 years Simcha Ronen and Oded Shenkar constructed eight categories identified as geographical regional clusters and placed nations within such spheres based on common attitudinal dimensions. Into a separate ninth category were placed those countries considered independent or possessing neutral cultural and work related values that did not fit the exacting blueprints of the others.[15]
  The list consisted of:

- Arab—*Abu Dhabi, Bahrain, Kuwait, Oman, Saudi Arabia, United Arab Emirates*
- Near Eastern—*Greece, Iran, Turkey*
- Nordic—*Finland, Norway, Denmark, Sweden*
- Germanic—*Austria, Germany, Switzerland*
- Anglo—*Canada, Ireland, New Zealand, South Africa, United Kingdom, United States (query as to Australia not included but it seems it would fit the criteria for this cluster)*
- Latin European—*Belgium, France, Italy, Portugal, Spain*
- Latin America—*Argentina, Chile, Columbia, Mexico, Peru, Venezuela*
- Far Eastern—*Hong Kong, Indonesia, Malaysia, Philippines, Singapore, South Vietnam, Taiwan, and Thailand*

* Independent—*Brazil, India, Israel, and Japan*

Using a pie chart, countries were placed in slices of geographical and ethnic denoted groupings due to their close exhibited shared cultural similarities. Those that exhibited more uniform patterns, a mix of cross-cultural determinants, additional work goals in respect to job satisfaction, managerial, and organization variables affecting fulfillment of job expectations as well as interpersonal orientations to such objectives were placed in closer proximity to each other. Ethnic origins and geographical proximity were also factored into the criteria. The closer the clustered slices were to each other the more these geographical groupings had in common.

Additional Research

Next to come along was the work of Terence Brake, Daniel Walker, and Thomas Walker devising a 10-point model developed to appreciate and work within international commercial situations.[16] They introduced four additional determinants:

- Competitiveness versus cooperation—individual combat-iveness as opposed to collaborative teamwork to create an environment of group harmony via common achievement. A qualified derivative of the previously noted Hofstede individualism versus collectivism.
- Private verse public space—separation of personal and communal duties/responsibilities as opposed to a common mixed open sharing of such dual elements in life.
- Deductive versus inductive reasoning—thinking patterns with one based on accepted demonstrated premises or rationaliza-tion as opposed to personal intuition or a feeling one has about something that cannot be easily explained.

Cogent reasoning versus emotional directed responses to issues.

- Contextual communication—degree to which message construction is dependent on the relationships between sender and receiver expressed as moving between a high versus a low context social environment dictating how thoughts via words and body language are conveyed between the parties.

This collection of cross-cultural value determinants sanctified and sustained the continuing pedagogy whereby the inspectional criteria is constructed on a versus spectrum; two diverse tendencies with a measured scale between them to determine a group's propensity to move toward one end or the other.

In 1998 Fons Trompenaars and Charles Hampden-Turner published *Riding the Waves of Culture—Understanding Diversity in Global Business.*[17] They introduced seven specific value dimensions as derived from three basic categories of inspection:

Relationships with People[18]

Universalism *versus* particularism—abstract societal codes applicable anywhere regardless of context to ensure equity and consistency as opposed to greater attention to special obligations brought on by special relationships and unique circumstances thereby allowing for flexibility and adaptation.

Individualism *versus* communitarianism—a prime orientation to the needs and wants of the self as opposed to an overriding consideration for the common goals and objectives to benefit the group.

Neutral *versus* affective emotion displays—suppressed, controlled, or subdued expressions of internal feelings as contrasted with open telegraphing of one's emotions via verbal or nonverbal (physical embodiments) behavior.

Specific *versus* diffuse—tasks are insulated and segregated from personal life as opposed to an integration of and permeation of all facets in one's life

Achievement *versus* ascription—in essence how status is accorded people in society. A doing group values constant individual accomplishments and skill usage whereas a being group accords value to an individual's birthright, education, and professional qualities, their experiences.

Attitudes Toward Time

Sequential *versus* synchronic—a series of nonintegrated passing events or an integrated and cross-influencing convergence of the past, present, and future to shape anticipated actions. Also relates to doing things one at a time in a logical order—single focused as opposed to handling many activities on a parallel basis—multifocus, all at one time.

Attitudes Toward Environment

Mastery *versus* harmony—exercising control by imposing one's will over nature versus going along with natural forces. Also relates to an internal driven society as opposed to one that responds to external pressures.

The Trompenaars model again set up diverse points or positioning reference, the *"versus"* syndrome, a recurring pedagogical approach to identifying the relative strength of cultural determinants on a society. Such generalized dichotomy was again relied on to calculate the relative movement of a group under an attitudinal cultural imperative placed under three umbrella terminologies. This approach, as the others before it, tended to label societies in an *either or* classification stigma; a black or white designation, a dangerous assumption. The degree to which they embraced one side or the other was negated and the ability for societies to exhibit characteristics or instances of both sides of the determinant pendulum was masked. Bridges of commonality, what societies might share as opposed to concentrating on their differences was inadvertently dismissed.

The latest authored work on the subject of cultural value determinants comes from the GLOBE (Global Leadership and Organizational Behavior Effectiveness) research program. Begun in the late 1990s under the direction of Professor Robert J. House at Wharton, the research was compiled over 10 years with results published in 2004. Using nine different cultural attributes and behavioral dimensions a team of 170 scholars correlated responses from 18,000 managers in 875 organizations based in 61 countries across three industry segments. The study was aimed to assess the societal cultural impact on leadership behaviors, attributes, and organizational practices. The GLOBE project identified the following nine cultural dimensions, borrowing from the work of previous researchers (six attributable to Hofstede) to identify and catalog cross-cultural leadership styles in response to such defined determinants:

- Uncertainty avoidance—degree of risk taking and ambiguous acceptance with a ***high or low*** designation
- Power distance—unequal degree of power and authoritarian acceptance in a society with a ***high or low*** designation
- Collectivism I: Social—degree of social practices to promote and reward the distributive use of group resources and collection action
- Collectivism II: In-Group—degree of individual expression of pride and loyalty to grouped institution to which they belong
- Gender differentiation or egalitarianism—extent to which a society accepts *or* minimizes role differences and gender discrimination
- Assertiveness—degree to which individuals are forceful, aggressive, and confrontational in social relationships with a ***high or low*** designation
- Future orientation—degree of individuals' ability/willingness to plan ahead and delay immediate gratification
- Performance orientation—degree to which society encourages and rewards group members for their contributions and achievements
- Human orientation—society's propensity to support and recompense individuals for being fair, altruistic, caring, and nurturing to others

The GLOBE model is a full-fledged measurement degree of cultural orientation and takes the subject from its beginnings as an inquiry into the simple handling of life's choices into a calculated assigned number of qualified numbered responses.

As one moves through the aforementioned chronological development of collections of cross-cultural value determinants the sets of applied inspectional criteria have gotten longer and more complicated. Many of the newer versions have been based on earlier research and could be characterized as expanding or perhaps linked to the theoretical positioning or facets tied to some of the original classifications. The common emerging denominator in all of these programs is the idea that [1] a duality exists in value determinant classification terminology—two alternating components each tied to the whole and [2] a measurement scale can thereby be erected between these two options to produce a relative positioning of one group to each other.

Derivative Cultural Determinants

Beyond the aforementioned collections of cross-cultural value determinants other researchers have proposed additional areas of inspection and generated some parallel and expanded factors to profile the human condition.

Edward T. Hill, an anthropologist, investigated and reported on three fundamental areas of cultural introspection.[19] His inspectional focus was based on the premise that culture was primarily a system for creating, sending, storing, and processing information in a format unique to specific groups. Although the theoretical approach underscored the powerful influence of culture on communication his classification models also relate to the framework, background, and surrounding relationship circumstances in which life and events take place. Language, one of the elements of communication alongside facial expressions and body posturing (both commonly referred to as body language), according to Daniel Everett is not related to one of the innate biological components of the brain as many linguists interpret it, but is an essential part of the set of cultural dimensions as its properties are uniquely shared by members of a particular group.[20] Simply put, language, oral, written words, and symbolic representations, is as culturally determined as are other mental and physical adaptations one makes in a uniform response to the environment around them. It should be noted that the Everett proposition, that a society's cultural begets its language, challenges the traditionally accepted biological roots theory of Noam Chomsky. First proposed in the 1950s it held that human language is governed by principles of universal grammar, a genetically determined capacity that imposes an identical fundamental shape on all the worlds speech.

Hall's analysis of cultural communication variables can be summarized as follows:

Context: Exchanging Messages/Other Discernible Traits

High context cultures—indirect, covert, and implied encoding and decoding with use of metaphors, flowery language and reading between the lines. Nonverbal with body language important./Relationship oriented with strong affiliations therefore collective and emotionally more intuitive. Formal with process more important them outcome. Time open and flexible.*

[Exemplified in the Middle East, Asia, Africa, and South America]
-versus-
Low context cultures—direct, overt, and explicit encoding and decoding with use of simple, open, concise, and efficient clear statements of intent. Very verbal with body language secondary./Task oriented with low commitment to affiliations therefore individualistic and rational. Informal with outcome more important then process. Time highly organized.**

[Exemplified in North America and Western Europe]

Time: Operation Use of

Monochronic—**doing one thing at a time, highly concentrated, prompt, task oriented/correlates with low context.
-as opposed to-
Polychronic—*doing many things at once, easily distracted, flexible, relationship oriented/correlates with high context.

Space: Proxemic Orientation

High territorial—boundary oriented, carve out personal space with concern for ownership/ correlates with low context
-or-
Low territorial—share space and ownership/correlates with high context

Theoretical Limitations

The aforementioned reviewed categorical dimensional collections from the noted research directed scholars have generated a number of theoretical approaches that are helpful in understanding culture. It must be noted however that no applied theory works perfectly. There are moments in time, contextual events, when one theory works better than another. But nothing works forever nor can it prepare or explain every cross-cultural encounter. Gaining an insight into one's own culturally influenced mind-set as well as that of another is no easy task. For centuries both spiritual and secular philosophers as well as the medical science of psychiatry have attempted to solve the riddle of how the mind works, what motivates and controls our behaviors, and what values we use in our relationships with others. The previously noted researchers in the field of commercial associations have added to the inspectional arena that looks to marry the overt, the physically evident, and the covert, the hidden or masked aspects of cultural faïence but in the end it is not an exact science. No absolute black and white distinctions can be made. Even with the tools such collections provide coupled with observational insight cross-cultural engagements are still a grey area.

With so many collections and subsets offered by researchers to explore and categorize cultural determinants a complicated matrix emerges. When these numerous cultural anthropological inspections are used in the classroom to help potential business students or are presented in executive seminars or as part of a program in predeployment training sessions for expatriates the ability to synthesize and then utilize them in their future international managerial positions is problematic. First, the massive arsenal of such inspectional guidelines becomes overwhelming to the point of exhaustive confusion. And second, almost all of them have a tendency to cause the user of such classification programs to view cultures in black and white terms exhibiting one end or the other of the qualified determinant applied. The problem with so many collections on cross-cultural dimensions as generated by renowned researchers in the field is that they *forsake the forest for the trees.*[21] Too much information tends to confuse issues not letting one see with clarity the overriding principle, the prime cultural curtain that hangs over all the others—collectivism versus individualism; the forest as opposed to the individual trees. The next section aims to unravel the Gordian-like cultural knot.

SECTION 2

Analyzing Cross-Cultural Determinants

Our differences pose a danger and only
learning not just what separates us but
what we share will bring us together.

CHAPTER 4

The Janus Pedagogy

The duality factor and continuum line of
cultural determinants is presented to allow for
an expanded understanding and applied
application for their use.

Almost all of the research collections presented in chapter 3 consist of two co-joined but opposite elements of the same cultural classification determinant. I call this the Janus principle, a nod to the ancient Roman two-faced god who is associated with doorways, beginnings, and transitions and represented as one who looks to both the future and the past. He has also been cited as a metaphor for facing opposite directions with one face looking eastward and the other westward, a separator of boundaries between two territories, a veiled reference to the East–West cultural divide described in chapter 2. It is interesting however that if one travels in either direction on the globe they will eventually get back to where they started, a physical phenomenon that exemplifies that even opposites have a commonality; together they form the whole. The term Janus-faced is also used to describe a person or a concept or designed approach that is duplicitous.

The idea that most cultural determinants are Janus-faced, composed of polar elements of the same defined term of inspectional classification is an important consideration to further the understanding and applied application of the methodology employed. The duality factor is paramount to understanding how different societies are constructed but is also the key to building bridges between them. The duplicity of mind-sets maintains that while a dominant or major cultural trait acts as the main controller over how one values, thinks, and therefore behaves, an underlying minor or subservient opposite exists within the same sphere of influence or defined cultural determinant. This semidormant characteristic is always present and can at times be activated to assume a contributing or even a limited controlling role in the specific determinant. In my article "The Gas Pedal and the Brake…Towards a Global Balance in Diverging Cultural Determinants in Managerial Mindsets"[1] this application was metaphorically exemplified by the use of the gas pedal and the brake in successfully moving and navigating a car; tantamount to guiding and controlling our culturally induced mind-set behavioral responses. The prime use of a car is movement, to propel it forward or backward, equal to one's actions in life. The vast majority of the time spent operating a vehicle is with the driver's foot on the gas pedal—this represents our majority determinant at work. As one engages other drivers on the road or environmental obstacles one needs to sometimes apply the brake to slow down or avoid an accident altogether. The process of maneuvering between and around others encountered on the roadways requires one to engage both the gas and brake pedals in a uniform symbiotic fashion requiring constant use of these dual mechanisms. This twin application can be a strong analogy to the recognition and use of cultural determinants in the business world while having equal application to the wider social global environment. To fully understand the proposition the philosophical concept of Yin and Yang is helpful.

Yin and Yang

To better explain and foster a more complete appreciation of the duality of cross-cultural determinants a conceptualized thinking approach based on Taoist and Neo-Confucian philosophy is a valued start. Taken from the *Taijitu*, which literally translates as a diagram of the supreme ultimate, the principle of Yin-Yang, as it is colloquially referred to, helps one to further understand the idea of duality. This philosophical representation defines the whole as composed of two counter balancing sides, both residing in the same structured entirety, and that therefore all things contain elements or traits that are opposite or different from the other half while embedded in the whole. The idea was first manifested in the teaching of the Chinese philosopher Laozi, the teacher of Confucius. The enlightened path, Laozi's dictum to peace and serenity, requires one to see both sides as conjoined and not separate. Neither can be complete without containing a piece of the other. The circle encompassing the two halves, the Yin and Yang parts, is indicative of the unity of the universe and hence all things, both tangible and intangible exist in a dual state. A bit or seed of each is found in the other, as depicted by the white dot in the black portion and a black dot in the white portion. See this imaginative symbolism and imagery as portrayed in Figure 4.1. In the construction of the numerous collections of cross-cultural value determinations as presented in chapter 3 the use of the terms "versus," "or," and "opposite" sets up a similar pedagogic approach by the original initiators of inspection and classification terminology and was sustained in the expanded versions.

Yin Yang, a Philosophical Chinese Language Example

Much debate amongst linguists centers on the Chinese word for crisis, *weiji* and the graphic symbol for the term being composed of two characters, danger, *wei* and opportunity, *ji*. The joining of these two distinct avenues of notice and action has symbolically been used by politicians and motivational speakers becoming part of public dialog to metaphorically represent a period, an incipient critical time when something important happens, a beginning or a change that can bring about good; hence the positive use of the word opportunity. Although a bit too much has been read into the word that simply means a dangerous moment, the idea that all is composed of a duality of conceptual elements well illustrates the Confucian philosophical behavior of people consisting of a yin and a yang. The Chinese word crisis really describes a tipping

Figure 4.1. Yin and Yang.

point between two balancing components, and the ability to swing either way depending upon the context of a situation. It is a good example to keep in mind to better understand and appreciate the numerous collections of cultural determinants that always have alternating references that are both contained with the same whole.

Duality Concept as Expressed in Other Cultural Philosophies

The idea that all things are composed of two alternating but contributing symbiotic elements is not only found in Far Eastern philosophical writing, but in the literature and religious foundations of many cultures around the world. The creation stories depicting the actual origin of mankind follow a similar theoretical discipline.

I once heard a learned Rabbi, during a discourse on the nature of natural love between man and woman, offer an explanation (a second reading) of the interpretation of the Hebrew *Torah* tale of human conception as presented in the second chapter of Genesis. It differed greatly from the normal widely accepted translation that God, when Adam fell asleep, took a rib out of his body and created a woman. His explanation of the event was that God initially created a singular human-like creature composed of both male and female elements but physically formed in God's image. He based his analysis on the fact that the translation of the Hebrew word *tsela*, does not necessarily mean rib but *side*. As in one side of the whole or sharing a common side, that is, picture Siamese twins; that in essence while the dual creature rested God split his creation in two dividing it into equal but separate beings, man and woman. And since that time they were destined to form continuing perfect unions as each could not live without each other longing to get back to their original state. The *Torah* in other portions claims that this is why man leaves his father and mother joining himself to his wife, and they become one flesh again. Adam does not necessarily correspond to a man's name as it literally in ancient Hebrew means "red earth," the clay from which God fashioned or molded the physical embodiment of mankind, beginning with a single entity. Even if this unorthodox rendition is rejected, the idea that man and women were created from a singular entity, such as Adam's rib, still embodies the principle that all things cannot be alienated from their collective spiritual essence when they were first united. A mutual yearning for each other still resides in both halves, the need for a Yin and Yang like balance in life and all things—the duality factor.

In Greek philosophy, Plato's dialog *The Symposium*, attributable to Aristophanes, tells of a fantasy in which the three distinct races of men (mankind) initially existed. It consists of males who inhabit the sun, a female residing on earth (a mother nature symbol or metaphor) and a third conjoining males and females living on the moon. It should be noted that celestial bodies played an important part in Greek and later Roman mythology. The last group, the congruent race, had four hands and feet, sides and backs forming a circle, one head with two faces with the balance of the body corresponding to such dual characteristics. Fearing the strength of such creatures and their threat to the supremacy of the Olympus dwelling gods, Zeus and Apollo cut them in half to reduce their imposing figure. But the two divided parts, sexual opposites, continued to desire the other with an overwhelming need to embrace each other both physically and spiritually, and form one unit again. The lesson of the allegory is that human nature was originally one embodiment and once split apart the craving to unite, to be whole again, is the love of man and woman. The tale also serves as a metaphoric image of all life, not just the physical but the mental as well, encompassing the spiritual as well as the secular, in essence a mythical restatement of Yin and Yang always present in the universe—the duality factor.

An Indian legend relates a tale before the beginning of time or precreation of human beings on earth. The universe is portrayed as consisting of a void or vacuum with only "the self" in the form of a human-like asexual being present. Upon discovering its own existence it first became afraid but realizing it was alone there was nothing to fear. As the story continues the self then experienced a different type of fear, a realization of its singular existence, and thereby longed for another to fill the empty space. The entity expanded its physical structure and split into two; becoming male and female. The male embraced the female, and begot the human race.

In these metaphorical depictions of creation of two sexual entities from the original one a complementary part of the other, their opposite, is retained in the resulting new one; they are forever connected even though separate. This principle relates to cross-cultural value determinants. While one side is more dominant then the other, a propensity to embrace a movement toward one side of a spectrum more than the other, societies still possess elements of their alternative acting as a counterweight, a persistent hidden brake on the prime governing strength of the other. The idea of maintaining a balance, the Yin Yang philosophical concept is also reflected in some religious doctrines. The founder of Buddhism, Gautama, taught that life is the pursuit of the Middle Way, essentially a path between the extremes of material worldliness and harsh self-denial of such pursuits in order to reach nirvana, a spiritual balance through the understanding of duality. To visually appreciate the duality imperative especially as it applies to cultural determinants take a look at the following picture (Figure 4.2). Upon initial inspection one's eyes will normally concentrate on the dominant dark scrip that reads ME. But upon closer focus the formation of the letters as viewed with the lighter background lets the word YOU emerge. Readers are asked to allow the author some literary license as beyond using the picture to exemplify the duality concept, the philosophical meaning or yin-yang inherent in the drawing, the evident joining of ME and YOU, was intentional.

The concept of duality beyond the cultural determinant linkage is also referenced in another context of differentiation between societies. Shaomin Li, whose theoretically researched concepts are referenced in chapter 7, states "Throughout the book, we will show that the

Figure 4.2. The duality of the self.

relationship-based governance system is distinctive and yet intertwined with its counterpart, the rule-based system, and the relationship between the two is complicated."[2] He is defining the two parts that make up the whole, the dark and the light that although entirely different comprise a day, itself a singular ingrained unit. The premises that every cross-cultural value determinant contains a contagious portion of alternating polar opposite conditions with elements of each thereby embedded in defining and applying the determinant is referred to as the duality factor. By recognizing that the dominant trait in one culture could marry its unequal or subservient characteristic in the other could two diverging cultures come together. In essence find common ground based on shared similarities. This phenomenon is well exemplified by the continuum line of opposing cultural determinants and the commonality all societies share.

The Continuum Line of Opposing Sides in a Cultural Determinant

To further illustrate not only the duality of cultural determinants but their operational influence on the human condition the idea of a continuum line is useful. A continuum line stretches or runs between two pillars of a cultural determinant. The opposing sides while representing alternative dispositions at both ends are indicative of a continuation inherent of the whole, not just one part or the other. The line drawn between the two represents the connection, the duality factor as stretched between the two opposing definitions of the specific determinant. It can show the degree of propensity within a singular cultural proposition—low or high, strong or weak using the "versus" criteria. Upon this continuum line a specific investigated societal or group culture could be plotted, indicating the extent to which they expressed a propensity to move toward one position or the other. In essence a gauge could be administered that allowed a more precise measurement scale of the degree of propensity to move toward one side or the other of a noted determinant. Instead of a fixed rigid absolute portrayal of a culture valued determinant in a society or group, that is, 100% one or the other, a number representing a relative position on the continuum could be established. Such a floating scale allowed researchers to compare the relative distance from the two opposing sides noting the distance separating them. A truer, more accurate device was created. It helps quantify the realization that while all cultures contain elements of both sides of the applied cultural determinant, the propensity to be dominated by one can be calculated and a measurable inclination to move toward either direction can be shown. Cultures could be plotted with an assigned propensity to gravitate toward either end of the continuum spectrum but it is all part of a commonly shared scale.

To visualize how this works consider the operations characteristics of a playground seesaw or teeter totter as depicted in Figure 4.3. The continuum board rests on a fulcrum that moves up and down based on the relative weight placed at either end.

When the seesaw principle is utilized to measure the degree of propensity for a specific determinant such Hofstede's individualism versus collectivism the resulting diagram would look like Figure 4.3.

As with the gas and brake example of the use of a cultural determinant each individual driver applies a varied degree of pressure on each of these separate devices that together help create successful movement of the car. Not all acceleration nor slowing down is at the same pace, each driver presses the gas or brake pedal with a different anticipated desire and hence result. We do not all move at the same speed even though we use the same joined instruments to achieve movement.

There is a decided and understandable inclination to label cultures in absolute terminology, that is, one likes to speed and the foot is always

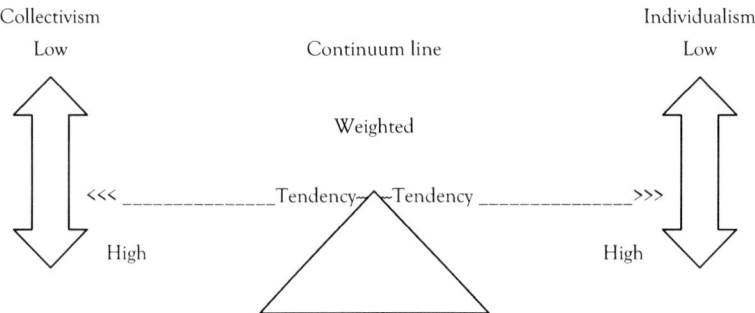

Figure 4.3. Continuum example: Seesaw or teeter totter.

on the gas pedal while the other is cautious and is always applying the brake. One tends to be placed in the propensity area depending on which side of the continuum they gravitate toward. Some national comparison tables don't use qualifying quantitative degree words like low, medium, or high designations but instead describe a culture in absolute terms, which side of the teeter totter do they fall on. For example, Hofstede's power orientation, the gauging of power distance, positions national cultures as either egalitarian or hierarchical, substituted terminology for the graduated extremes of high or low.

Paul Cartledge, a contributor to *The Ancient Economy*, not to be confused with the previously referenced Moses Finley treatise of the same title notes that societies exhibit "heterogeneous pluralism, in economic life as in other fundamental aspects of both individual and communal activity."[3] He reminds us that a society's approach to providing life's needs contains and combines aspects of individualistic and collective cultural determinants, that such Yin and Yang elements are equally needed to attain and maintain one's existence and that both exist in all of us.

The Continuum Line

Understanding that all determinants are merely points on the continuum line allows one to appreciate that a respective passive collaterally opposite piece also exists, further illustrating the duality factor. As depicted in Figure 4.4 based on the assigned values in Table 4.1 country numbers are plotted on the range field that stretches between the two poles of the determinant as defined by percentages as well as descriptive words. This analysis, using the determinant individualism as opposed to collectivism, ranges on the scale from 6 for Guatemala to 91 for the United States indicating a span of 85 points on the continuum line. The fulcrum point, the middle of the teeter totter between these two polar sides of the determinant is 42.5 or 43. Recognizing this tipping point allows for a more definitive national classification to emerge of a specific country's propensity to shift to one side or the other. For example, the Arab world at 38 is closely positioned toward the center 43 and would calculate at 45% individualistic (38 divided by 85) while 55% collective. The region is not as highly collective as normally portrayed but more balanced straddling the

Hofstede's Collectivism versus Individualism

Collectivism   Individualism

6 <<<<<<<<<<<<<<<<<<<<<<<<< <<<<43>>>>>>>>>>>>>>>>>>>>>>>>>>>>>91

^

< Middle Range Fulcrum >

__(1)___(2)_(3)_ (4)___(5)___(6)___(7)_(8)_(9)_(10)__(11)___(12)___(13)___

Numerical scaled points versus word descriptions of specific countries: Ref: Table 4.1

(1) Guatemala / 6 (7%), Ecuador / 8 (9%) and Panama / 11(13%) – *Very highly collective*
(2) Singapore / 20 (24%) – *Highly collective*
(3) Chile / 23 (27%) – *Highly collective*
(4) Hong Kong / 25 (30%) – *High to moderate collective*
(5) Greece / 35 (41%) – *Moderately collective*
(6) Brazil and Arab World / 38 (45%) – *Collective balanced with slight collective tendencies*
(7) Japan / 46 (56%) – *Determinant in balance, with slight individualistic tendencies*
(8) India / 48 (57%) – *Determinant in balance, with marked individualistic tendencies*
(9) Spain / 51 (60%) – *Moderate movement toward individualism*
(10) Israel / 54 (64%) and Austria / 55 (65%) – *More moderate movement toward individualism*
(11) Germany / 67 (79%), Norway / 69 (81%) and Ireland / 70 (82%) – *Individualistic*
(12) Italy / 76 (89%), New Zealand / 79 (93%) and Netherlands / 80 (94%) – *Highly individualistic*
(13) Great Britain / 89 (105%), Australia / 90 (106%) and United States / 91 (107) – *Strongly individualistic*

Figure 4.4. Selected country plotting scores on a continuum.

Table 4.1. Country and/or Regional Values for Four Hofstede Dimensions

Country	PDI	UAI	IDV	MAS
Arab world	80	68	38	52
Argentina	49	86	46	56
Australia	36	51	90	61
Austria	11	70	55	79
Belgium	65	94	75	54
Brazil	69	76	38	49
Canada	39	48	80	52
Chile	63	86	23	28
Columbia	67	80	13	64
Costa Rica	35	86	15	21
Denmark	18	23	74	16
Eastern Africa	64	52	27	41
Ecuador	78	67	8	63
El Salvador	66	94	19	40
Finland	33	59	63	26
France	68	86	71	43
Germany	35	65	67	66
Great Britain	35	35	89	66
Greece	60	112	35	57

(*Continued*)

Table 4.1. Country and/or Regional Values for Four Hofstede Dimensions—(Continued)

Country	PDI	UAI	IDV	MAS
Guatemala	95	101	6	37
Hong Kong	68	29	25	57
India	77	40	48	56
Indonesia	78	48	14	46
Iran	58	59	41	43
Ireland	28	35	70	68
Israel	13	81	54	47
Italy	50	75	76	70
Jamaica	45	13	39	68
Japan	54	92	46	**95**
South Korea	60	85	18	39
Malaysia	**104**	36	26	50
Mexico	81	82	30	69
Netherlands	38	53	80	14
New Zealand	22	49	79	58
Norway	31	50	69	8
Pakistan	55	70	14	50
Panama	95	86	11	44
Peru	64	87	16	42
Philippines	94	44	32	64
Portugal	63	104	27	31
Singapore	74	**8**	20	48
South Africa	49	49	65	63
Spain	57	86	51	42
Sweden	31	29	71	**5**
Switzerland	34	58	68	70
Taiwan	58	69	17	45
Thailand	64	64	20	34
Turkey	66	85	37	45
United States	40	46	**91**	62
Uruguay	61	100	36	38
Venezuela	81	76	12	73
West Africa	77	54	20	46

*Bold numbers indicate the highest and lowest scores for each dimension.
Source: "A Culture Survey," (1997), retrieved September 14, 2001 from: http://www.css.edu/users/dswenson/ web/culture/cultratings.htm Activity based on Geert Hofstede's research on cultural differences. *Promoting a European Dimension of Intercultural Learning - Developing School Materials* EFIL Seminars, Vienna, Austria, April 17–20 and Lisbon, Portugal, June 26–29, 1997.
PDI = Power Distance; UAI = Uncertainty Avoidance; IDV = Individualism, as opposed to Collectivism; MAS = Masculine, as opposed to Feminine.

continuum line between individualism and collectivism. Countries like Japan and India, often referred to as being strongly influenced by Eastern collective philosophies, are in fact also close to the 43 degree fulcrum point, scoring at 46 (54%) and 48 (56%) respectively, leaning toward individualism but retaining a 46% and 44% proclivity to be collective. The relative balance portraying the yin yang relationship exists and the duality factor is well illustrated.

A plotting of the scores from Table 4.1 for individualism versus collectivism on the continuum line is presented in Figure 4.4. This diagram allows one to visualize the relative distance of selected countries moving away from the fulcrum or tipping point. It also helps to view the positioning of countries relative to each other. The raw scores from Table 4.1 are noted and in parenthesis are the individualistic percentages they would generate based on a 85-point span separating the lowest and highest values for collectivism versus individualism.

Degrees of Duality

The relative scores for the various Hofstede defined dimensions (see Table 4.1) are too often used to indicate a propensity to tilt, per the teeter totter illustration (see Figure 4.1) toward a pronounced one side or the other of the specific cultural determinant being calculated. Hence cultures are characterized as possessing a high or low power distance and risk avoidance or tilting toward masculine versus feminine or being more individualistic as opposed to collective. These measured degrees are not absolutes but indicative of a relevant positioning across the measurement scale, the continuum line (see Figure 4.4), a propensity to shift toward one side or the other.

What must be respected is that every scored country has a corresponding duality, a major and minor element to the cultural dimension being measured. Recognizing the counter balancing of these dual contributing factors, the relative strength of each dual determinant can be an effective tool in working with a new culture.

If one comes from a more decidedly individualistic society, like the United States at 91, the top of the scale, and needs to address those in the Spanish culture at 51 they match up well with 48% of that population, but need to keep in mind that there exists a slightly noticeable segment, 52%, that is collective. On the other hand, if an American manager engages a Guatemalan associate scoring 6 or 7% (6 divided by 85—range of points from 6 to 91) individualistic and a corresponding 93% collective it will be harder to assimilate into their culture. But there is room to tap into the acquiescent minority side of a specific dimension. This docile lesser percentage is the crack in the cross-cultural wall that allows one to search for a wedge of similarity upon which to build relationships. Instead of concentrating on the differences that separate cultures one needs to look for avenues of commonality. While it is prudent to recognize diversity it is equally important to search for and embrace connections of shared aspects of each one's unique culture.

The V Distortion Factor

The plotting of the assigned scores of value determinants across a continuum line (Figure 4.4) has inadvertently produced a V configuration as the demarcation line separating the polar sides of cultural dimensions causes a prejudicial distortion to take place. The divide or V Factor, as evidenced by the surveyed numbers assigned in Table 4.1 emerges if one simply grabs the fulcrum point and pulls it down to form a V configuration (Figure 4.5). Countries falling on the same segment, right or left side, (Figure 4.5—A or B) forming the arms of the V tend to be defined and associated with the same general classification of the determinant evaluated. The result is evidenced by the language descriptions used to ascribe different societies as exhibiting high or low tendencies for the Hofstede determinant collections such as power distance and uncertainty avoidance or their designation as individualistic or collective as well as masculine or feminine. Those countries falling on opposite arms of the V (Figure 4.5—A or B) are more statistically dissimilar and the further up the separated arms of the V one proceeds the greater the disparity as a wider cultural distance or gap exists—how far apart they are. For example, the cultural determinant collectivism versus individualism shows a very wide disparity between Guatemala at the top of V arm A, decidedly collective society, and the United States at the top of V arm B, definitely individualistic. However, Brazil and the Arab world close to the bottom of V arm A thereby fall in the collective designated side compared with India

Collectivism (A) versus Individualism (B)

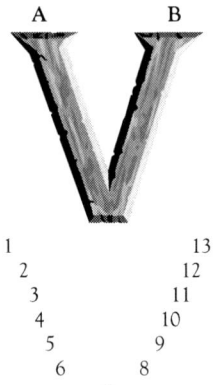

(1) Guatemala / 6 (7%), Ecuador / 8 (9%) and Panama / 11(13%) – *Very highly collective*
(2) Singapore / 20 (24%) – *Highly collective*
(3) Chile / 23 (27%) – *Highly collective*
(4) Hong Kong / 25 (30%) – *High to moderate collective*
(5) Greece / 35 (41%) – *Moderately collective*
(6) Brazil and Arab World / 38 (45%) – *Collective balanced with slight collective tendencies*
(7) Japan / 46 (56%) – *Determinant in balance, with slight individualistic tendencies*
(8) India / 48 (57%) – *Determinant in balance, with marked individualistic tendencies*
(9) Spain / 51 (60%) – *Moderate movement toward individualism*
(10) Israel / 54 (64%) and Austria / 55 (65%) – *More moderate movement toward individualism*
(11) Germany / 67 (79%), Norway / 69 (81%) and Ireland / 70 (82%) – *Individualistic*
(12) Italy / 76 (89%), New Zealand / 79 (93%) and Netherlands / 80 (94%) – *Highly individualistic*
(13) Great Britain / 89 (105%), Australia / 90 (106%) and United States / 91 (107) – *Strongly individualistic*

Figure 4.5. V Factor—Diverging numerical scaled points:
Ref: Table 4.1.

close to the bottom of V arm B sliding into the individualistic side. Using absolute terms like collective and individualistic representative of the V separation factor distorts the small difference between these nations as they are really more similar in their cultural make-up with regard to this specific determinant. This is the danger of sweeping generalizations and the desire to place absolute designation or labels on societies without recognizing the element of degrees.

This misapplied distortion of the continuum line destroys one's ability to appreciate the naturally occurring duality of opposing sides inherent in all value determinants, drawing one's focus to separation instead of shared latent characteristics. It strengthens the divide concept by obscuring the dormant part of a value determinant in favor of placing a presumptive label of a society on its more active dominant partner. It also fails to recognize that even within the two segments making up the V configuration (Figure 4.4—A or B) variances of degree positioning exist. The V factor hijacks the yin-yang element so important to cross-cultural understanding, the conceptual duality bridge that joins alien cultures.

Reliability Issue—Statistical Disconnect?

While many sets of cultural value classifications have been promulgated based on the work of researchers in the field as chronologically presented in chapter 3, the practical use and application of such determinants or dimensions requires surveys to determine which side of the defined spectra societies fall on. As one reviews the quantitative survey results using a variety of cultural determinant measurement statistics they would be well advised to consider the Albert Einstein observation that "Not everything that can be counted counts, and not everything that counts can be counted." [Note: Some attribute this quote to William Bruce Cameron and his 1963 book *Informal Sociology: A Casual Introduction to Sociological Thinking*, (1964), New York, NY, Random House.] The number values assigned in such measurement to arrive at quantified appraisals do not always represent absolute qualification of how a society behaves or in fact will actually behave in respect to the criteria employed to define a cultural determinant. Table 4.1 is such an assessment and although it is used in this text to extract and demonstrate some postulated principles one needs to remember that all surveys contain a sampling error. To make estimations about a population, a given society, statisticians use a random sample representative of the entire population. A sampling error or confidence level occurs when the sample results deviate from the "true" population value. Normally, the sample size determines the magnitude of the margin of error. The larger the sample size the smaller the Standard Error, which is typically expressed as a percentage variance, that is, give or take X%. Without getting into the mathematical dynamics of sampling error calculations, a commonly accepted formula based on the re-expression of the sample size, Confidence Levels of 95%, 90%, and 80% are most normally used. Therefore any statistical survey is not absolute in its results and those relying on them are cautioned not to accept them as unconditional.

When Hofstede, in the mid-1960s, developed his initial four dimensions he based his findings on a limited sample amongst specific nationalities. He surveyed IBM employed managers, a unique class of individuals, sharing perhaps an educational or professional culture and an organizational culture by nature of their common employment positions; the 3rd and 4th steps in culture building as previously presented in chapter 3. While the Hofstede dimensions, as noted earlier, are the most widely referred to theoretical classifications of cross-cultural determinants it is questionable if they are transferable to the wider population of a country given the principle of statistical error. If one justifiably assumes that IBM managers in a nation represent a very small percentage of the total population then the Standard Error possibility is expanded. This is not to say that the classification system used is incorrect; just that its application to represent the "true" population value is suspect.

Given this consideration and applying a Standard Error factor of just 5% the country scores for all determinants in Table 4.1 could be recalculated. While the normal medium for all determinant scores would result in a median of 59, adjusting for a 5% Standard Error could cause this median to swing or deviate by as much as 2.95 points (+/– 5% of 59 = 53 or 59). [Note 59 is the mid range between the lowest or 5, Swedish masculinity and the highest 112, Greek uncertainty avoidance.]

If one rounds off, for example, to a factor of 3 error points the previously denoted V factor split becomes questionable. A country like Austria, which scored 55 points on the individual dimension scale, ever so slightly toward collectivism, could presumably be adjusted to 52 or 58 causing it to tilt one way or the other with a presumably incorrect assumption without application of the margin error recognition. If the Standard Error percentage is increased then interpretations of such a survey maybe doubtful. Those countries that fall at the higher ends of the spectrum as the scale runs from 6 to 112 would have their results less impacted by the Standard Error consideration. It is therefore suggested that such survey results be used as a general guide, evidence of propensities but not absolute determinants of expected culturally induced behavior.

Another result of the Standard Error element is that it flattens out the sharp contrast of the V Factor (see Figure 4.5) of a cultural determinant producing a softer U Configuration (see Figure 4.6). The strong varying

(1) Guatemala / 5–7, Ecuador / 7–9 and Panama / 11–13 – *Very to Highly collective*
(2) Singapore / 20–24 (24%) – *Highly collective*
(3) Chile / 22–27 – *Highly collective*
(4) Hong Kong / 25–31 – *Moderate collective*
(5) **Greece / 31–39 – Slightly collective**
(6) **Brazil and Arab World / 38–46 – Balanced with slight collective tendencies**
(7) **Japan / 41–51 – Balanced, with slight individualistic tendencies**
(8) **India / 44–53 – Balanced, with slight individualistic tendencies**
(9) **Spain / 46–56 – Balanced with slight movement toward individualism**
(10) Israel / 49–60 and Austria / 50–61 – *Moderate movement toward individualism*
(11) Germany / 67–80, Norway / 62–77 and Ireland / 63–77 – *Individualistic*
(12) Italy / 66–84 (89%), New Zealand / 71–87 and Netherlands / 72–88 – *Highly individualistic*
(13) Great Britain / 80–98, Australia / 81–99 and United States / 82–100 – *Strongly individualistic*

Figure 4.6. U Configuration/V factor adjusted for standard error of + / – 10%.

differences in the V arms are replaced by a wider arc in the U and the stark separation is leveled out at the bottom if the Standard Error is raised to 10% (see Figure 4.6). The duality factor becomes more evident and more important as definitive variances are blurred when the assigned country table values are adjusted to account for the Standard Error percentage. More countries move toward a middle or balanced range between opposing sides of a cultural determinant and the parallels in societies using this dimension are more noticeable.

A Better Method to Appreciate the Relative Strength of a Country's Determinant

Recognizing that two cultures possess elements of each other others dominant or minority positioning of the same determinant allows one to tap into their dormant side and match it up with the majority side of another society. Such repositioning provides common ground to build bridges of commonality between presumably diverse cultures.

However instead of using the whole numbers as presented in Table 4.1 replacing the whole numbered ratings with a percentage allows one to better grasp the relative values assigned to the cultural determinant of a specific country or region. Recalculating Table 4.1 ratings based on a point factor of 85 on the continuum line, the range separating the lowest score 6 and the highest 91 for all countries and regions tabulated in the survey for individualism versus collectivism, a percentage, 0% to 100% emerges (see Figure 4.7).

Using a percentage indicator to mark the relative positioning of the whole numbers in the survey allows for a quicker more efficient method to compare cultural determinant propensities. The tendency to tilt toward one end or the other of the determinant spectrum, be it a defined characteristic like individual as opposed to collective or a high or low aspects of singular characteristic like power distance is more precisely revealed across a more pronounced perception field when applying percentage measurement scale.

For example, a Danish businessperson whose society is prone to be individualistic at 74 per Table 4.1 actually falls into the 87 percentile, a better indicator of how strong they individualistic tendencies are. They can tap into their limited 13% collective proclivity to match up with the highly collective propensity of an Indonesian at 84% whose individualism is measured at 14 (Table 4.1) restated at 16% (see Figure 4.7).

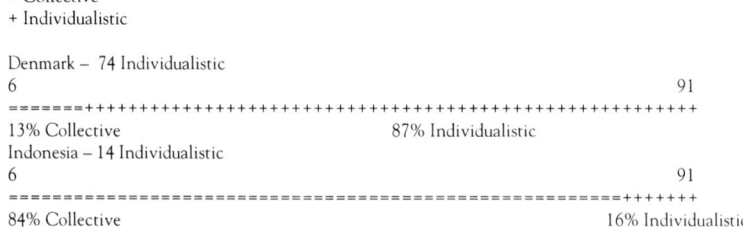

Figure 4.7. *Percentage representation of Table 4.1. whole number ratings.*

Even countries that fall (are plotted) on a similar sides (median < 43 >) of the continuum spectrum can be better analyzed, i.e. Germany at 67 is individualistic but not as much as Australia at 90. per Table 4.1. But when recalculated to their actual percentage of 79% and 106%, respectively, a better understanding and appreciation of their strength as to their relative positioning as culturally individualistic emerges. Likewise Pakistan at 14 is collective as is Singapore at 20 per Table 4.1. When recalculated to their actual percentage 84% and 76% the severity of their respective collective disposition is more clearly revealed.

Not only does this closer evaluation process allow for a more precise positioning on the continuum scale but it also allows for the comparison of cultures, via countries, as to how far apart they really are to each other in a given dimension even if they both fall within the same V factor positioning model moving up 0% to 50% on one side and 50% to 100+% on the other side.

For example, while the South American countries of Guatemala, Ecuador, Panama, Chile, and Brazil share historically inspired cultures the first three are more highly collective, 93%, 91% and 87%, then Chile at a more moderately collective 73% and Brazil that just barely crosses over into the collective category at 55%.

Japan, India, and Spain that have no or little common historically linked cultural background no less share a geographical location, all on or near different continents.

Their numerical factors per Table 4.1 are respectfully 46, 48, and 51 but when recalculated to produce a percentage evaluation as regards a propensity for individualism, 54%, 56%, and 60%, a clearer determination emerges.

CHAPTER 5

Filtering the Cultural Determinant Milieu

Cutting through the cultural minutiae
created by numerous researchers and
their lists of value determinants. The
search for a prime cultural nucleus.

As previously reviewed in chapter 3, numerous collections of cross-cultural value determinants help define and explain various cultural differences with each set of research proposed theoretical determinants containing their own criteria. A comparison of such lists indicates that many are closely aligned with each other or merely substitute new terminology for a previous one or graft on to an existing phraseology. Trying to keep in mind all of these models is a hard task for the educated academic researcher and/or the professional cross-cultural instructor to master, and even more so for those first exposed to them. It is difficult to select which collection or specific determinant is best to use in a given situation.

To cut through the maze of available material and narrow the field it may just be possible to sort out the wide spectrum of alternative cross-cultural values to select few fundamental determinants and then filter this codified smaller group out to arrive at a singular key denominator on which all are based. This is the pedagogy we will apply to the vast collections of cultural determinants previously noted. In essence we will be applying the theory of Occam's Razor to the complicated matrix in order to comb through and separate out a prime controlling determinant.

Occam's Razor

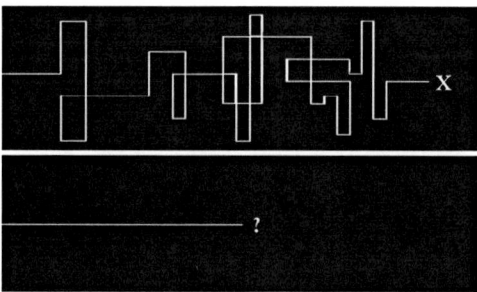

Figure 5.1. *Normal cultural matrix navigation versus Occam's Razor approach.*

The 14th-century English logician and Franciscan friar, William of Ockham, postulated that the explanation of any principle should make as few assumptions as possible, eliminating those that make little or no difference in the observable predictions to explain the hypothesis or theory investigated. The concept is often expressed to sustain the idea that no elaborate solutions should be offered where simple ones will suffice; a "rule of thumb" caveat. In Latin the presumption is known as ***lex parsimoniae***, the "law of parsimony or succinctness" leading to the underlying statement that entities must not be multiplied beyond necessity for understanding and appreciation of the principle to be illustrated and hence applied. A similar approach is attributed to the logic of Socrates by Xenophon (circa 430 BC). Known as the Socratic method, it is a persuasive technique built on generating a series of inquiries leading one to a singular, sometimes paradoxical conclusion. This pedagogical approach is also reflected in a maxim often attributed to Leonardo da Vinci advising that simplicity is the ultimate sophistication.

While the suggestion may seem rather trivial, it admonishes one to choose from a set of otherwise equivalent models, the numerous collections of cultural determinants, to explain a presented concept in its simplest explanatory form, in essence to shave down complex constructed ideas to a central or dominant theme from which the other variables or constructs emanate. It is not as radical as being unable to untie a knot by simply cutting it apart with a sword, a reference again to Alexander the Great and the Gordian knot (the legend by which one supreme ruler of Asia would emerge), but the approach is practical. The less abusive Occam's Razor application allows for global managers to acquire a concise workable set of cross-cultural indoctrinations with less chance of confusing the multiple theories that often result in inconsistencies, ambiguities, and redundancies. If one applies this analytical approach to sets of cultural determinants, where an infinite number of possible models have been offered by researchers to explain and thereby categorize social behavior and attitudes, a cleaner, more pronounced vision to observe and deal with cross-cultural issues emerges.

Using the principle of Occam's Razor it is hypothesized that an inspection of the numerous collections of cultural determinants (as noted in chapter 3) first produces a set of four basic cultural elements; and that upon further examination one prime fundamental determinant emerges that is central to the growth and maintenance of the others; that this chief cultural determinant influences and is therefore engrained in the others, acting as a core nucleus for their construction.

To visualize this pedagogical approach imagine a wagon wheel (Figure 5.2). The circumference is made up of all of the numerous collections presented in chapter 3. Like spokes on a wheel, four basic determinants radiate out from the center to support the outer circle. In turn, these fundamental structural components rest on a core singular birthing denominator.

Figure 5.2. The cultural wagon wheel.

It is proposed that the four key spokes are:

1. Power distance
2. Uncertainty avoidance
3. Individualism versus collectivism
4. Time perception.

The centerpiece upon which all is constructed is ***individualism versus collectivism***. This value determinant appears in most studies either as a pure repetitive consideration or is offered in an alternate defined format. It is the key determinant providing a social centerpiece that all others are constructed upon and is therefore the launching pad for cultural anthropology as applied to the commercial sector. It is the tool to untie the proverbial cross-cultural knot. A two-level straining approach will be used in this analysis.

The first level in this process is a re-inspection of the previously introduced collections of value determinants, in chapter 3, to uncover the four initial spokes on the wheel. The second level is a finer filtering to arrive at a core cultural determinant.

1st Level—Common Linkages Amongst Research Generated Collections

A review of the aforementioned theoretical collections offered by learned researchers reveals that many can be dissected and traced to the proposed four basic cultural dimensions.

Kluckhohn Revisited

Two of Kluckhohn's five dimensional inquiries fall within the purview of the individual versus collective orbit. He labels the construction of a society with its emphasis either on serving the individual or the group's collective good, as *relational orientation*, simply an umbrella term for a society having a propensity for individualism or collectivism. The definition of *activity orientation* has an individual versus collective ingredient. A difference is noted in cultures that value separate accomplishments or divided achievements—an individual-based imperative. On the other side are those cultures that value ascription, status accorded one dependent upon their relationship with others, an inspectional approach requiring a collective group imperative, such as family heredity, educational institution, professional association, etc. Mankind's orientation to the natural world around them from subjugation, to harmony with or mastering conditions one comes in contact with correlates to one's social environment. Power distance is the acceptance of those in control (high degree), like nature's elements, or the ability to challenge and alter (low degree) such circumstances. It is also comparable to uncertainty avoidance, the reluctance to alter conditions due to fear of failure (high degree) versus risk taking (low degree). Kluckhohn also included temporal orientation, a past, present, or future point of reference, which is one of the proposed four basic dimensions.

Condon Revisited

Condon, while including many of Kluckhohn's inspectional criteria, adds *social mobility* and *social formality*. Both refer to the ability of one, the individual, to move freely, take risks, and proceed in society unencumbered by class or caste distinctions, a distinctive group versus individual identification factor as well as a descriptive reference to characteristics embedded in the exercise of power distance and risk uncertainty. Both his references to *gender dominance* and *dispersal of authority* have aspects of individuality and collectiveness to them, as well as elements of power distance and risk uncertainty. Equality of the sexes and democratic principles have individualism at their roots due to the egalitarian concept being applied. Notions of male hierarchy and authoritarian power require an organizational or group structure to allow for such institutional construction, hence a decidedly collective based indicator as opposed to individuals acting alone.

Hofstede Revisited

Hofstede's initial four-dimensional collection with the fifth added later, in recognition of Asian inspired time reference, has formed the basis for researchers in the field for many years. As noted before, many sets of value determinants have both grafted on and expanded Hofstede's initial work compiling sets and subsets of these baseline inspectional parameters.

The Hofstede collection specifically cites *individualism versus collectivism* as one of the original four dimensions and retains it as part of the basic four. *Uncertainty avoidance* is measurement of a risk factor that is controlled by stricter rules and regulations for the group to follow—the need for a collective behavioral system whereas the opposite consideration, the acceptability of the unknown, the ability to take higher risks in one's life is an individual gamble targeting each separate person in a society. This dimension is also one of the four basic determinants.

Power distance is again based on an egalitarian orientation or in essence a recognition of equality amongst all people, an individually based concept (each man is endowed with inalienable rights of freedom not to be restricted by group directional mechanisms). The opposite side requires a submissive hierarchal structure, which again needs a collective group configuration to be recognized and utilized forming the third member of the basic four.

Hofstede's *masculine–feminine* terminology has troubled cross-cultural researchers with many proposing that a better designation would be materialism versus emotional nurturing values in life. This semiobscure reference has an individual versus collective origin as masculine societies are characterized by individual material value accumulation as opposed to group sharing. Even such "Beat the Jones" mentality—an American colloquial reference regarding an individual's desire to accumulate more or do better than one's neighbor has a collective element to it. It requires an individual's accomplishment to be measured by group based value elements, the accomplishments of others around them. A masculine based determinant also has a decidedly high risk-taking element attached to the process as venturing forth on one's own without the aid of others means taking chances. Feminine societies favor intrinsic altruistic values, the nurturing of relationships with those one comes in contact with, a group motivational consideration. A feminine determinant directs people to stay within accepted group norms and hence not take chances, a low risk taking profile for the individual. The masculine versus feminine determinant also exhibits diverging elements of traditional hierarchy systems, a condition associated with low and high power distance acceptance.

The masculine individual induced achievement motivation tends to challenge those in power in order to achieve their own personal ends (low power distance). A feminine culture tends to be more accepting of group denoted leadership to promote harmony and hence exhibits a high power distance element.

In essence the masculine versus feminine determinant exhibits many of the nuances found in Hofstede's first three dimensions and needs to be dismissed as redundant. Its basic ideas are contained in the other three initial determinants and the sexual identification directive merely is an extension of the others.

As noted earlier Hofstede added to the original four dimensions a *long-term versus a short-term outlook—time orientation*. Such inclusion, evidence of the reflected importance he placed on it, increases its value as an element to be considered and hence part of the group of the four fundamental determinants. While this dimension seems to be outside the realm of interpersonal relationship construction it could be argued that aspects of it are reflective of and influenced by the individual mind-set as opposed to collective thought. As noted later, individual-based societies tend to concentrate on achievements in their lifespan, more closely driven to value time in a limited quantities. Collective cultures are more traditionally based carrying such values across and between generations thereby expanding their time horizons both forwards and backwards.

Brake Revisited

The Brake model of cultural determinants includes *competitiveness versus cooperation*. This designation is affiliated with individualism as opposed to a collective orientation of a society. At its core to be competitive is struggle or enter into a rivalry between two persons, to do battle with another individual opponent. While groups can engage in such uniform events, the initiative of one who proceeds to organize others in a similar pursuit, the individual is the paramount driver or initiator of the group activity. Cooperation on the other hand entails working or acting together for a common purpose or benefit, a decidedly group harmonistic endeavor that begins and ends in a group environment. Competition also entails a combative feature or risk advertence component.

It also alters the power distance element in a society as one emerges as a winner over others. The fundamental determinants, individualism versus collectivism, power distance, and uncertainty avoidance risk are all affiliated with and act as underlying drivers in competition versus cooperation.

Private versus public space invites a comparison between personal, separated, or a decidedly departmentalized arena for the individual as opposed to the communal sharing with those around us in respect to our life and daily activities, a group relationship process requiring a more pronounced collective agenda. It can also be used to collaterally define power distance as a low classification results in acquiescence to public egalitarian space while a higher power distance results in private spaces attributable to one's place in an organizational hierarchy.

Trompenaars Revisited

Trompenaars dimensions begin by re-labeling individualism versus collectivism by inserting the term *communitarianism* for group involvement. *Universalism versus particularism* separates the need for abstract common codes of socially induced group behavioral guidance with the opposite need to handle obligations and responsibilities on a more one to one basis, with the need for more separate flexibility and attention paid to specific individualized considerations.

Specific versus diffuse is a refinement of Brake's *private versus private space* wherein tasks are separated or insulated, an individualistic approach as opposed to an integration into a variety of grouped tasks. *Achievement versus ascription* revisits Kluckhohn's *activity orientation* and falls back on the underlying premise of the value of individual accomplishment in contrast to one's value as identified by their associations or group belonging. It contains a measurement of power distance in a society, as it is attributable to either individual achievement or group pronounced ascription. Even *neutral versus affective* can be traced to a society where individuals keep their emotions in check as opposed to sharing them with an external audience—the group. *Attitudes toward the environment* are a restatement of the Kluckhohn inspectional mythology, to be subservient to or desire mastery over life around us. It relates to risk taking, to either challenge or accept the circumstances around one, as well as power distance accepting nature as a dominant force or deciding that mankind can determine to change it.

GLOBE Model Revisited

The GLOBE cultural incorporates Hofstede's original four models; (1) uncertainty avoidance, (2) power distance, (3) collectivism, split into two parts, (a) institutional collectivism and (b) in-group collectivism (4) gender positioning or traditional masculine versus feminine based societies and its alter ego (5) human orientation, to oneself or others. Such categories need not be revisited, as except for gender positioning dismissed earlier in the discussion of the Hofstede use of the terminology they are all part of the four basic determinants. However the division of collectivism should be noted. Institutional collectivism is defined as "the degree to which organizational and societal institutional practices encourage and reward collective distribution of resources and collection action."[1] In-group collectivism is defined as "the degree to which individuals express pride, loyalty, and cohesiveness in their organizations or families."[2]

The terms 6 *assertiveness* and 7 *performance* orientation have been added to the list with 8 future orientation completing the list of nine investigative (two collective subdivisions, an a) and a b) attributes. The *assertive* factor is an indication of an individual's degree of confrontation in respect to one's engagement of people around him. In essence it is a desire to measure whether one integrates in a harmonious fashion with regard to their social relationships with others or maintains an individualized singular aggressive style to promote and receive personal gratification. As such it has a strong element of individualism versus collective overtones embedded into it as well as power distance and uncertainty avoidance.

The definition of *performance* is a dimension criterion aimed at measuring how a society encourages and rewards group members for organizational improvement. In essence it is indicative of whether a society places value on the individual or the group with regard to activity contributions, again evidence of an individualism versus collective root. Human orientation investigates the degree to which individuals technically have collaborative or group oriented characteristics—to assist and work for the improvement and benefit of others, a measurement of involving others in their life the collective imperative.

Hall Revisited

High-context cultures are grounded in strong pronounced interpersonal relationships that make definitive and important distinctions between the in-group and out-group; that is, family and outsiders. Trust building is of paramount importance. Affiliations direct and control actions and reactions in high context cultures. Those cultures falling into this category are strongly associated with a pronounced relationship orientation with others as found in determinant classifications such as those exhibiting high power distance, placement in a collective society with feminine overtones while associated with high risk avoidance, and past orientation to determine acceptable behavior. A high-context culture coincides with Trompenaars ascription dimension as one's actions are dictated by positional status within a group.

On the other hand, low-context cultures mirror societies that can also be described as low power distance and risk avoidant, individualistic, more masculine, and having a future orientation. Hierarchies and social positioning do not determine behavior and people are encouraged to speak their mind even if it means challenging a superior. As such those in low-context cultures have low uncertainty avoidance, they take chances viewing the assertiveness of the individual as paramount to the harmony of the group. High- and low-context cultures in essence are based on and reflect composites of the four basic determinants offered at the first inspectional level of the filtering process.

The aforementioned comparison of various research generated cultural determinants indicates that many repeat, overlap, or contain the ingrained nuances that are associated with the four basic dimensions. Trying to avail all the determinant collections offered by these learned and respected practitioners can be confusing leaving those desirous of a cross-cultural indoctrination becoming disillusioned and desirous of a simplified limited list. What emerge are four basic cultural determinants:

- Individualism versus collectivism
- Power distance
- Risk tolerance
- Time orientation.

Applying Occam's Razor Filter Further

Following the initial filtering of the multitude of cross-cultural determinants to arrive at a few workable components, let us move to the second step, a final straining to arrive at a prime or singular controlling value dimension that influences all the others. Having whittled down to ostensibly the Hofstede collection, minus masculine versus feminine, a further application of Occam's Razor allows us to pare down the focus to the simplest axiom, one key cultural indicator.

2nd Level, In the Quest for a Singular Cultural Dimension

I have attempted to follow the instructional pedagogy beginning the process in the prior section with a comparison of the numerous cross-cultural dimensions collections looking for common denominators, level 1. At this point we move onto level 2 using a mathematical deduction and then a further theoretical inspection. The first uses survey results previously presented in chapter 4, Table 4.1.

The 59-Degree Deviation Factor

Using Table 4.1, assigned values from this survey applying the four commonly accepted Hofstede cultural determinants, one observes the lowest number registered on the applied measurement scale is 5 (Sweden at 5 for Masculine) and the highest number is 112 (Greece at 112 for Uncertainty Avoidance). The average of these values equates to 58.5 and is rounded to 59 for mathematical illustration. This medium value is designated as the middle of a continuum line (see Figure 4.2) on which the assigned values for a particular determinant could be plotted. Given the separated distance from this pivot point or fulcrum balance base (see Figure 4.1—teeter totter) the propensity degree or weight to tilt one way or the other could be more accurately determined for an investigated determinant. Its strength or how deeply it impacted a national culture, relative to the other determinants could thereby be gauged.

The further the original assigned numbered value moves away from the base number 59 the stronger that determinant registers as the deepest or most ingrained in a society. Table 5.1 presents the results of this formulated application.

The resultant numbers were calculated by the difference between them per Table 4.1 and the number 59. For example in the Arab world a score of 80 for PDI results in a deviation factor of 21 (80 <> 59 = 21) while a score of 38 for IDV produces a deviation factor of –21 (59<>38 = 21) Whether the number is shown as positive or negative is irrelevant. It just indicates moving toward or away from one of the dual aspects of the defined determinant. The highest resulting value across all four determinants for each country and/or region is present in bold number (note two territories had a tie in the calculation so the results are shown in bold italics). For example, in the Arab world plus 21 under the PDI column shows a propensity toward a high power distance acceptance and the minus 21 under the IDV column shows a marked propensity away from individualism and toward its opposite collectivism.

Table 5.1. 59 Axis of Deviation, Measuring the Relative Strength of Specific Determinants in Countries: Ref. Table 4.1

	54 responses	52 countries
Individualism v. collectivism	26/48%	26/50%
Uncertainty avoidance	12/22%	12/23%
Power distance	10/19%	10/19%
Masculine v. feminine	6/11%	6/12%
Total	54/100%	52/104%*

*Actual number of countries surveyed was 52 but 2 countries had identical scores for two determinants so percentages were calculated using actual responses, 54 and number of countries, 52.

Actual results tabulating the major or dominant determinant, as shown in bold type on Table 5.1, irrespective of the whole number or negative designation are:

Respondents to this survey indicated that the deepest impact on their culture, as measured by the largest variance from the median, was individualism versus collectivism; 48% and 50%, respectively, depending on overall responses or countries. This determinant was equal to almost all the others combined. It is the most ingrained and most strongly felt of all the four determinants used in the survey, emerging as the chief cultural dimension.

Further Evidence of a Correlation, a Pattern of Integrated Effect

Beyond the previously demonstrated mathematical analysis, the 59-degree factor, are there any other numerical correlation patterns between the determinants that give rise to anointing individualism versus collectivism as the base ingredient? Possibly yes. Again referencing Table 4.1 those nations scoring high on individualism produce corresponding equal results in the three other dimensions.

IDV/PDI Correlation

Cultures that score a high value for individualism have a marketed tendency to have a lower value for power distance. With the exception of Belgium [75 individualism/65 high power distance] and France [71 individualism/68 high power distance] 98.79% of those countries scoring high on individualism scored low on power distance. This overwhelming statistical imperative could be attributable to the fact that individualism supports egalitarianism as opposed to a hierarchical society.

IDV/UAI Correlation

With regard to a correlation between individualism and low uncertainty avoidance, 12 nations out of 152/7.89% did not match a propensity for individualism with a high value for low uncertainty avoidance but 92.11% did. Individuals take risks more easily as they see it as gaining a personal reward.

IDV/MAS Correlation

As to the influence of individualism on masculine orientation, 16 nations out of 152/10.53% did not match a propensity for individualism with a strong masculine identity—but **89.47% did**. Individualism supports a more masculine oriented society based on task achievement and material accumulation as opposed to the feminine characteristics of relationship development and interpersonal nurturing, traits associated with a collective orientation.

Table 5.2. VARIANCE VALUES, *Deviation from Median*
59 Country and/or Regional Values for 4 Hofstede
Dimensions: Ref. Table 4.1

Country	PDI	UAI	IDV	MAS
Arabic World	21	9	–21	–7
Argentina	–10	27	–13	–3
Australia	–23	–8	31	2
Austria	–48	11	–4	20
Belgium	6	35	16	–5
Brazil	10	17	–21	–10
Canada	–20	–11	21	–7
Chile	4	27	–36	–31
Columbia	8	21	–46	5
Costa Rica	–24	27	–44	–38
Denmark	–41	–36	15	–43
Eastern Africa	5	–7	–32	–18
Ecuador	19	8	–51	4
El Salvador	7	35	–40	–19
Finland	–26	0	4	–33
France	9	27	12	–16
Germany	–24	6	8	7
Great Britain	–24	–24	30	7
Greece	1	53	–24	–2
Guatemala	36	42	–53	–22
Hong Kong	9	–30	–34	–2
India	18	–19	–11	–3
Indonesia	19	–11	–45	–13
Iran	–1	0	–18	–16
Ireland	–31	–24	11	9

(Continued)

Table 5.2. VARIANCE VALUES, *Deviation from Median*
59 Country and/or Regional Values for 4 Hofstede
Dimensions: Ref. Table 4.1—(Continued)

Country	PDI	UAI	IDV	MAS
Israel	−46	22	−5	−12
Italy	−9	16	**17**	11
Jamaica	−14	**−46**	−20	9
Japan	−5	33	−13	**36**
South Korea	1	26	**−41**	−20
Malaysia	**45**	−23	−33	−9
Mexico	22	23	**−29**	10
Netherlands	−21	−6	21	**−45**
New Zealand	−37	−10	20	−1
Norway	−28	−9	10	**−51**
Pakistan	−4	11	**−45**	−9
Panama	36	27	**−48**	−15
Peru	5	28	**−43**	−17
Philippines	**35**	−15	−27	5
Portugal	4	**45**	−32	−28
Singapore	15	**−51**	−39	−11
South Africa	*−10*	*−10*	6	4
Spain	−2	**27**	−8	−17
Sweden	−28	−30	12	**−54**
Switzerland	**−25**	−1	9	11
Taiwan	−1	10	**−42**	−14
Thailand	5	5	**−39**	−25
Turkey	7	**26**	−22	−14
United States	−19	−13	**32**	3
Uruguay	2	**41**	−23	−21
Venezuela	22	17	**−47**	14
West Africa	18	−5	**−39**	−13

PDI = Power Distance.
UAI = Uncertainty Avoidance.
IDV = Individualism, as opposed to Collectivism.
MAS = Masculine, as opposed to Feminine.
Bold indicates strongest deviation factor in a particular country and/or region: Italics a tie
Source: Based on the pedagogy of Table 4.1. "A Culture Survey," (1997), retrieved September 14, 2001 from: http:/www.css.edu/users/dswenson/web/culture/cultratings.htm Activity based on Geert Hofstede's research on cultural differences. *Promoting a European Dimension of Intercultural Learning–Developing School Materials* EFIL Seminars, Vienna, Austria, April 17–20 and Lisbon, Portugal, June 26–29, 1997.

Conclusion

Educational practitioners as well as those consultants and trainers offering advice on cross-cultural indoctrinations might begin by offering a base or prime dimensional factor, **individualism versus collectivism**, as the central driving determinant in a society. Once this parameter of investigation is settled, and the propensity of a cultural group can be identified as either moving toward individualism or collectivism, a statistical pattern of probability for the emergence of other related dimensions can be argued, with exceptions. Individualism versus collectivism is the most strongly felt determinant of the four determinants as measured in Table 5.1 and gives rise to or engineers the emergence of the three other determinant tendencies. It is at the center of the cultural wagon wheel, as previously illustrated, and thereby allows for the construction of the other three spokes that in turn support the wheel's circumference; one's cultural defined identity. Use of the applied philosophy of Occam's Razor to compile a short collection of cultural dimensions and arriving at one controlling dimension to assist in the evaluation of a society should not be taken as a negative or threat to the inspired work of the cited researchers. It is merely proposed that using individualism versus collectivism as the prime initiating determinant enables managerial commercial practitioners, as well as introductory students, to have a clear and concise starting point to appreciate and understand cross-cultural engagements. It is proposed that individualism versus collectivism is the prime idée fixe of our psyche. It determines our identity and all other determinants emerge from this programmed chief controller of our life.

Theoretical Examination of Individualism versus Collectivism as the Lead Determinant

A further investigation into each of the theoretical conceptual approaches sustains the basic proposition that a majority of aforementioned collections have embedded in them a common base element, individualism versus collectivism.

As the four proposed determinants are based on the pioneering work of Geert Hofstede it is prudent to again review his activities on constructing his collection. As noted in chapter 3 he traveled the world in the 1960s and 1970s interviewing managerial employees of a then, and even now, major multinational, the IBM Corporation. Using detailed questionnaires, Hofstede inquired into how people solve problems and how they work with others in order to gain an insight into their basic attitudes, values, and behavioral actions; in essence, their culturally induced mind-sets with a commercial environment. From such a vast and comprehensive database he constructed a series of common dimensions with applicable rating scales. His collection of cultural dimensions is even today the most widely used paradigm in examining and comparing cross-cultural psychology. The Hofstede model of inquiry, although based on limited or closed commercial network of respondents as opposed to a wide social survey, has found its way into the more generally accepted theoretical approach to the science of psychological analysis. Even nonfiction books like the popular and bestselling *Outliers, The Story of Success,* by Malcom Gladwell incorporates the Hofstede collection to explain and shed light on the reactions and relationship determinations of pilots in an airline crash.[3] In fact, the series of stories and anecdotes related in the Gladwell book have as their underlying premise the influential capacity of "cultural legacies…. on our twenty-first-century intellectual tasks"; how our mind-sets are constructed and used.[4] Using the four basic cultural determinants let us further trace the influence and controlling nature of the prime determinant individualism versus collectivism on them.

Time Orientations and Perceptions

Many of the cultural dimensional collections include a reference to a time orientation or perspective. Some express the subject as pure time value such as the American clock is king axiom "time is money" and to waste or mistakenly hoard it is productively wrong as if it is capable of being quantified or measured in missed financial opportunities versus the notion that time is an unlimited resource and that events transpire in a steady rhythmic pace. Others place the time element with an "on time" reference with punctuality versus lateness in terms of the acceptance a society exhibits for delays, cancellations, and postponements. Still others place time orientation as the degree of attention to the past, present, and future. (See Hofstede, Trompenaars, GLOBE), while some show its effect on thinking patterns and procedural approaches to determinations. Hofstede's original list of cultural dimensions did not include a time reference but he later added it, perhaps in recognition of the influence of the teaching of Confucius on the behavioral mind-sets of Far Eastern cultures. The driving principle of his ideas is the search for what was good in the traditions and practices of the past and to use such guidance to determine actions in the present, which in turn sets the stage for the future. Whichever defined approach is taken in respect to time the subject has a direct correlation to individualism versus collectivism. Individualism with its focus on the person as opposed to the group is an egotistical perspective. The individual can influence life as "where there is a will there is a way." The individual can change and improve the environment, mastery versus subrogation or harmony. The hardworking individual can accomplish any objectives. Hence time is an element to be controlled and used effectively to accomplish such personal goals. The American refrain "let's get down to business" as time is a waste'n sums it all up. An individualistic culture therefore is deeply time sensitive. It must be used or it is lost. Goals are measured by exacting on-time schedules. The present can be managed to influence the immediate future, while the past cannot be adjusted.

Collectivism, with its focus on the group, takes a more flexible view of time. It is associated with multiple wider obligations that influence individual based time perceptions. The responsibilities one has to others, family, and friends or numerous membership associations may alter or prevent things being tied to an exacting time reference, as one has to take or abide by other considerations. One's individual initiative may be governed by role and status in a group and hence one's ability to manage and control time is limited. Age and grade within a group environment trumps one's ability to do things at a pace they determine. Generation measurement of goal attainment combines the past and present as groups transcend time as opposed to an individual's eventual demise as one does not live in the past and there is no future beyond one's time on earth. Time orientations may contain a correlation to the base factor, individualism versus collectivism, as the propensity to associate oneself with the past requires an affinity to look back at a period when one did not exist. To accept or give credence to customs and traditions that prior groups developed, accepting such mores as potentially controlling or influencing their actions today—a collective historic imposed imperative as opposed to a present or future orientation that the individual can control. A pronounced affinity to take the long view is a condition of collective societies as the common good, one that affects all, needs time to mature. Asian and Middle Eastern cultures talk of riches to flow in the future based on current activities with their children inheriting the fruits of their labors. Those in an individualistic environment have a more pronounced short-term orientation expecting more instant results from their current endeavors. Their horizons are more limited with a pronounced focus on their own lifespan.

Time perspective also affects the way we think. While some physicists have postulated that time might not be expressed in a linear equation such as past, present, and future but all intertwined in space and occurring simultaneously, some cultures seem to exhibit this theoretical phenomenon. Collective cultures with a strong transgenerational group orientation take a composite approach incorporating all three time spaces in their deliberations. Current events are built on past ones while what is decided today affects the future. All activities encompass traditional approaches based on ancestral linkages. Their thinking incorporates such practice as exemplified by a circular and in some cases a looping matrix in their procedural approach. In meetings, such societies begin anywhere, jumping around the points on a circle or the numbers on a clock. They start with point F or 6 o'clock, then move to point C or 3 then to point J or 10. Some begin with A or 1 o'clock, move on to B or 2, then C or 3 then loop back to A or 1 again. This conflicts with a linear progression of A, B, C or 1, 2, 3; a point being concluded, then the next one following in order mostly practiced by individualistic cultures.

Power Distance

The term power distance is associated with a society's view and therefore acceptance of authority in their lives. It is deeply connected to how strongly a person can voice their opinion that may be in disagreement with those in a superior or controlling position over them. It has been associated with egalitarianism or social equality and its opposite social inequality that affords special status in a society be it age, older being respected and granted privileges, to those more highly educated, to those that are part of a particular majority including race, creed, or religious persuasion. It has even been attributed to the subservience of women to men in certain societies. The dimension also helps to determine individual initiative versus holding back and not challenging those in predetermined roles of granted authority or positional status. It is instrumental in explaining why in some societies the best qualified person should be granted responsibility and authority to get things done versus time in grade, family, or friendship relations and other culturally prejudicial considerations based on custom and tradition like the eldest son running things upon the demise of the family patriarch. It affects decision making with a person in the know contributing useful information versus deferring to those in recognized authority, an ascription based society. Collective societies have a marked tendency to embrace high power distance while individualistic societies champion low power distance feeling that all can and should have an equal voice. Where groups predominate a society the need for a recognizable hierarchy or organizational pecking order needs to be established so the institution can properly get things accomplished. Unquestionably following orders given by a superior is tantamount to good social behavior and the proverbial individual nail that sticks out will be pounded down or torn out of the group. Subordinates do not see their job as helping to resolve problems in organizations. They show little or restrained individual initiative respecting the decisions of their superiors and follow their lead. The comment by a Korean linguist sums up high power distance by stating "All social behavior and actions are conducted in the order of seniority or ranking; as the saying goes, *chanmul to wi alay ka issta*, there is order even to drinking cold water."[5]

Individualism breeds competition, personal ambition, and performance-based assessment as opposed to simply following orders and therefore the harmony of the group may be challenged without leaders in charge. Individualism empowers people to do whatever is necessary to get the job done whereas collectivism with a high power accent attached to it prevents various kinds of work from being done. Activities may be accorded low or high status; and some work may be considered below one's dignity or place in the organization where other work is considered above one's station and their title does not permit them to do the job. At the core of power distance and driving a society's proclivity for its high or low degree is individualism versus collectivism. Individuals have a strength and inflated ego that challenges those in authority. On the other hand, collective types operating in a group need to assign leadership. Their existence in the unit is dependent on a uniform moving of the group toward common goals that require stronger adherence to a pronounced or emerging authority that cannot be constantly challenged or the group will stagnate or come apart.

Risk Uncertainty

The question of how well a specific society deals with risk, exhibiting a high or low tolerance for ambiguity in life was first approached by Hofstede. Behind this definitive definition lies a multitude of connected components. On a generic societal plane this cultural dimension is also said to pertain to those accepting of the status quo and those opposing it. The dimension is deeply connected to change acceptance and rule following. Those adverse to change feel it should be accepted passively and not sought after while those embracing change view it as breaking the rules or stepping outside of agreed boundaries. High-risk societies always like to know what is expected of the individual as determined by acceptable group defined expectations.

Collective societies tend to exhibit a lower risk uncertainty than individualistic societies, as any alterations may affect the harmony and maintenance of the group, which are paramount to preserving it. Individualistic societies are more prone to take risks, and pursue change as they see this as a constant progressive effort to dynamically increase value and efficiencies. Individualism sustains the premises that one can influence the future by stepping out of the proverbial box and taking chances. Collective societies see life as following a preordained course or set of rules and what is good for the group is good for the individual. Collectivism and individualism deeply influence risk taking. Individuals tend to go it alone possessing a higher degree of confidence. They take risk as the rewards from such adventures accrue directly to them. Collective societal units form groups just so they can avoid risk taking—sharing the risk.

Masculine versus Feminine

The designation of masculine versus feminine to signify alternating cultural values in a society is perhaps, as previously mentioned, the most misunderstood and hence misapplied of the Hofstede constructed dimensions. The terms are not related to any Freudian sexual connotations or psychological interpretations of men and women as derived from their differing inherent physical characteristics. Rather the words are used to denote and convey value variances. The masculine side symbolizes a preoccupation with the materially measured aspects of life normally associated with work goals. Hence monetary reward or earnings from one's labors or creations and societal advancement using wealth attainment as a gauge are conditions associated with a masculine culture. Individual competition and conflict are more readily acceptable aspects of life. On the feminine aspiration meter the formation, nurturing, and sustaining of private personal relationships takes precedence over overt material gain. Family interests are stressed over professional aspirations. Harmony of the group takes precedence over individual goals. Group integration is stressed in a feminine society as opposed to individual achievement at the expense of the collective needs of others.

The masculine versus feminine designation is also used to further exemplify cultures that harbor conservative or traditional viewpoints as to the role of men and women in society as opposed to a more liberal view of the mixing of functional responsibilities or positions of the two groups in daily activities. A masculine orientation provides for very distinct tasks to be assigned with men working at labors outside the home and women staying at home caring for the children. Men are the proverbial breadwinners providing for the material well being of the family unit while women cultivate and nourish relationships in the family entity.

The male is primarily responsible for offering protection from environmental dangers and providing physical sustenance while the female maintains the intimacy of the cloistered domestic setting.

Individualistic societies gravitate toward more masculine values while collective societies tend to be more feminine oriented. Masculinity in the Hofstede definition is deeply concerned with the pursuit of quantifiable personal goals—individual achievement and independence thereby deriving their identity from themselves. Femininity focuses on interpersonal relationships and the welfare of others that produces a quality of life—collective group.

Individuals tend to line up well with masculinity whereas collective societies are more comfortable with feminine values. Nurturing and empathetic traits are reflective of caring about others, that the welfare of the one is dependent on group harmony.

The Chicken or the Egg?

If individualism and collectivism act as the prime determinant from which all other emanate which came first and perhaps germinated the other? As Joseph Campbell comments in his chapter introducing differences in the East and West, "It is not easy for Westerners to realize that the ideas recently developed in the West of individual, his self-hood, his rights, and freedoms, have no meaning; whatsoever in the Orient."[6] The same statement could be made of those in the East, that they cannot easily comprehend the Eastern value placed on the individual in society. Campbell goes on to note that individuality had no meaning for primitive man and that the concept was alien to the civilizations developing in Mesopotamia, Egypt, China, or India.[7] These ancient societies viewed and therefore defined human beings by a group affiliation as evidenced by one's identification as belonging to a clan, or tribe. As civilization progressed other forms of common or shared assemblage often denoted by race, creed, religion, and even geopolitical positioning morphing into national citizenship emerged. While some may argue under the Occidental revelation that mankind is directed to attain its highest potential, a kind of nirvana in the Buddhist traditional spiritual thinking, a shift in focus to the individual needs to take shape not withstanding that humanity is portrayed as initially begining as a collective effort. One is reminded of the heavenly nature of the natural order that the sun always rises in the east but sets in the west. Is this a metaphorical illustration that mankind rose as a collective society but over time became individualistic?

If one subscribes to the spread theory of mankind, that one singular society begot all the others around the world presumably beginning on the African continent, then how do we arrive at such pronounced cultural splits around the globe that seem to be tied or classified with reference to their eastern and western geographical locations? Frances Fukuyama, author of *The Origins of Political Order*,[8] like many writers explaining how societies organized themselves, does answer the chicken or the egg question, which came first—individualism or collectivism. Clearly mankind's natural development, and for that matter all species on earth, began by being collective. Man and almost every living creature with the exception of the one cell organism, the amoeba, mate to reproduce. In doing so a multiunit is formed—the immediate family, male, female, and offspring. While the family form can take on many characteristics, from multiple partners to monogamy, the need to reach out and touch others of one's kind is universal. The process does not stop at the singular family unit but produces a clan or tribe at the human level and the pride, herd, colony, flock, at the animal and insect stage while in the plant vegetation category, a similar forest, garden, or plain. Things on earth seem to naturally come together although there is the occasional singular entity of any of these groupings in a solitarian setting.

On the Other Hand

It can be postulated however that the collective initiative really masks a state of cooperative individuality, that in order to achieve one's individual goals a group conduit was utilized. As individuals strive to accomplish their selfish goals such action occurs in a social context, so all attainments are conditioned by their context. Any individual's achievement should therefore be considered entirely derivative from society and without the collective efforts of those around one nothing would be accomplished. We all join organizations not so much for wanting to work with others but for the system it offers that allows individuals a structure on which to build their singular aspirations. Like a building that rises it allows one to reach the utilizing platforms of assent—other people. Students in academic institutions are taught that group projects allow them to learn and approve their skills but in the end each receives a grade or score for their efforts. In life just as in business the same principle applies. One rises to the top utilizing the collective labors of those they have formed relationships with.

Merging Individualism and Collectivism

Mankind, from the investigation of our earliest beginnings banded together driven not just by the sexual motivated drive to procreate, but also survival. The need for protection against nature's elements of destruction, both other humans and beast predators, caused people to band together. The inherent desire to sustain oneself, find basic nourishment and shelter in a hostile environment drove people to form extended families beyond the man–woman conjugal unit creating clans and tribes to procure common requirements. A simplified division of labor also resulted in improving the lives of those that lived together as early man learned that when alternating personal skills were combined a mutually satisfying system evolved that in turn gratified individual desires. Collectivism was not only a human shared experience but is inherent in all creatures. As earlier noted, land animals in prides, packs, herds engage in shared exercises as they forge and hunt for food in groups while banding together to warn each other of danger and ward off attackers. At rest they also form unified protective enclaves. Ocean creatures exhibit the same ingrained instinct to work together. Even earthly vegetation in all forms, although subject to climatic conditions of temperature and terrain, tends to growth in uniform allotments. All earthly species form alliances; it is the engrained physical natural order of life.

Outside of the corporeal need driver Robert Trivers also proposes a mental component to the collective order of things. According to a theory he calls reciprocal altruism, the human endeavor to act kindly toward strangers is based on a learned as opposed to instinctive human response to one's actions. Because our ancestors over time and the aggregate received an individual quid pro quo benefit from acts of generosity our first reaction upon engagement with an alien party is to offer friendship, from relationships, as the result tends to be positive.[9]

In *The Righteous Mind* by Haidt, a social psychologist, concludes that our mind set is primarily attributed to the individual versus the collective dichotomy.[10] That societies do not start with individual but originate with the group because such development is associated with the cosmic sequence of all things. Living alongside others prizes order and not equality. Interdependence not autonomy drives our values and influences the individual decision-making-process. Forms of individual action need to be suppressed as self-expression weakens the social fabric of the group. Therefore societal relationship divisions in the world, cultural differences, are the primary result of the individualism versus collectivism dimension.

It would seem that all humans following nature initially possessed an instinctive leading collective requirement toward others that was entrenched via their adaptive attitudes toward those they came in contact over time, the educational factor. The balance struck between the primeval collective imperative with the trailing individual spirit, a latent dormant part of mankind, has always impacted and controlled our behaviors; and is at the core of cross-cultural development. But a question still lingers. How did some societies and their dominant trait collectiveness move closer to individualism as the chief driver of their lives? Why did some cultures embrace this new direction, personal fulfillment, while others steadfastly held on to the original prevailing definer of their society, collectivism? Why do these distinctly different determinants both allow for the respective societies practicing these dual characteristics to live in a circle of social harmony and prosperity? But when such dramatically different groups reach out and engage each other why is there a natural attempt to impose either way of life on the other? Is there a middle ground that allows them to coexist, metaphorically speaking a merging of eastern and western values or did such alternating values always exist in such diverse societies as previously proposed? A restatement of the yin yang duality comes to mind. Societies dominated by a collective or individual initiative do allow their alternative subservient cultural determinant to emerge as a positive force in the development of their civilizations.

Traditional National Identities Rebuffed

Man's desire to run and organize his daily affairs, the management of one's labors in respect to his environmental resources in order to sustain and improve life, is perhaps the best method of inspection to draw introspections into cross-cultural determinants. It can be used as a bridge to bring cultures together as examples of the two spheres or duality of specific cultural determinants can be shown in all societies—the dominant and the subservient are not always what they seem.

China, Clearly Collective?

An inspection of rice production in China, itself perhaps one of the most collective societies on earth, reveals an underpinning of individualism. The cultivation of rice, the main staple in the diet of Chinese citizens, is a process begun in ancient times over 4000 years ago. It continues today in its unabated original design system with marginal changes, with the process accounting for a large percentage of the country's agricultural industry, itself utilizing close to 65% of the national labor force. Rice production is so important to Asian cultures that oftentimes the word for rice in a particular Asian language also means food itself.

The difficult and arduous task in the preparation and cultivation of rice in paddies is based on ancient traditions still practiced today. The successful cultivation and harvesting of rice depends on the singular knowledge and ingenuity of the individual farmer and his organization management of his closely knit family of properly instructed helpers.[11] The process is very environmentally sensitive with the skill of the seasoned individual farmer paramount. While the Mao period saw the use of people's communes with mandatory sales of crops to local state purchasing stations with strict rationing limiting rice consumption, today small family farms working private plots, of which there are many, are free to sell or consume what they grow. Even within the traditionally strong collective Chinese social environment there is a cultural legacy tied to individualism as evidenced by the centuries old sayings of peasant farmers. They consist of motivational phrases[12] all tied to the individual imperative as opposed to collectively directed references:

- "No food without blood and sweat."
- "Farmers are busy; farmers are busy; if farmers weren't busy, where would grain to get through the winter come from?"
- "In winter, the lazy man freezes to death."
- "Don't depend on heaven for food, but on your own two hands carrying the load."
- "Useless to ask about the crops, it all depends on hard work and fertilizer."
- "If a man works hard, the land will not be lazy."
- "No one who can rise before dawn three hundred sixty days a year fails to make his family rich."

The underpinning of the decidedly collective Chinese society is the individualistic initiative as shown by rice farmers with this spirit in modern times visited on the surging growth of China's commercial entrepreneurs. While the strength and solidarity of the Chinese people has always been reflected in their collective ability to overcome adversity and is exemplified in the historic construction of the Great Wall (referred to as the Long Wall by the Chinese) over three generations, it is also a nation whose individuals invented gunpowder, printed paper and print currency, the compass, and a host of other scientific breakthroughs. In China individualism has always dwelt alongside collectivism.

United States, Clearly Individualistic?

While individualism is deeply associated with the United States the historic Western expansion and development of the country was a testament to the collective efforts and collaborative spirit of the pioneers. The settlers who went West were rigid individualists but cognizant of the dangers of traveling across hostile and treacherous terrain of which they know little about they chose to travel in group, that is, wagon trains. Even after they reached their separate destinations and set up their individual farms they relied on their neighbors to help them construct their homes and livestock quarters. The traditional barn raising is a collective event during which a community, men, women, and children all come together to assemble a barn for one or more of its neighbor households. As such newly developed areas were sparsely settled or on the edge of the no man's land frontier, it was not possible to hire carpenters or other professional tradesmen to construct such needed infrastructure. Therefore participation was mandatory for community members to survive. All able-bodied members of the community are expected to attend but were not paid for their valued services. Failure to attend a barn raising without the best of reasons could lead to community censure and the casting out of the individual. The practice was widespread particularly in the farm belt of North America during the 18th to 19th centuries. Despite traditions of independence, self-sufficiency, and refusal to incur debt to one another, all exemplifying cultural individualism, community barn raisings were a part of life in the history of the United States. The process occurred in a social framework of cross-relationship building with a good deal of interdependence and collectivism being used.

Members of rural communities often shared family bonds going back generations built on economic necessity. They traded with each other, buying and selling land, labor, seed, cattle, and the like. The idea of collective activity carried over to worshipping together and celebrating family events together even though a spirit of individualism drove them to initially leave their homelands and immigrate to the United States. The portrayal and even statistical conclusion that Americans are highly individualistic masks the fact that elements of collectivism are incorporated in this culture's make-up. The idea of teamwork to get something done is inherent in the American culture from sporting events to commercial endeavors.

The duality of opposing sides of a determinant, like individualism versus collectivism as noted in the comparison of China and the United States, resides in all cultures. While one side may dominate, aspects of the alternative are always in play. When encountering a society that exhibits a dominant or latent determinant of one's own culture the ability to match up is always there.

Managerial Implications Using Individualism Versus Collectivism

A clear indication of individualism versus collectivism is well illustrated in the following anecdotes and short cases within a business environment.

Employment Practices

Example 5.1

When employees of American and Japanese firms are asked what they do, an inquiry into their work status, Americans normally respond with "I work for" so and so company while their Japanese compatriots reply "I belong to" this firm.

The culturally induced differences in their answers well exemplify how they view relationships in life's choices. The American response is indicative of a definitive personal separation from the group with the accent on "work for" while the Japanese counter with "belong to" demonstrates a strong affiliation to be identified personally with the group as opposed to individually. In individualistic cultures people view themselves as independent agents who use their private skill sets and abilities as a "have gun will travel" consideration.[13] Their loyalty is fleeting and goes to the highest bidder causing them to movie around a lot in their organizational career choices. In group oriented collective cultures one sees their private social value as reflective of their association with the organization they belong to. Loyalty is thereby important as it signifies their existence. Without it they are lost. They tend to stay with one company throughout their commercial career envisioning the relationship as almost like a family that they owe their allegiance to.

Example 5.2

An Indian subsidiary of an American MNE was experiencing extraordinary growth. It was decided to preempt future needs by quickly hiring additional personnel. In a follow-up meeting between the

(Continued)

American regional director and the country manager the local executive was proud to provide an alphabetical listing of newly hired employees to show he had complied with headquarters' directive. A scan of the names oddly revealed that most bore his surname. When the coincidence was questioned he proudly pointed out that they were all extended relatives. Upon being reminded of the company's policy on the danger of nepotism and the principle of hiring the most qualified being the prime criteria for employment he was a bit taken back. He noted that tradition in India demanded that families have a responsibility to look after each other but more importantly loyalty to an organization is more important then the skill sets that can be taught. By hiring those that he already had a close relationship with, he knew them better than strangers, he could trust them, and such individuals would always be loyal to him and therefore the company. Once taught to handle job requirements they would not leave for better pay or promotion, company retention rates would remain high, and the investment in training would pay off in the future. Unlike American employees who constantly bounce from one company to another to further their individual career goals the Indian collective system containing an ingrained loyalty was a better method to ensure continuing and sustained company success.

The collective nature of the Indian society is clearly illustrated in this example with the importance of relationship loyalty attached to decision making in the hiring of personnel. Notwithstanding the dangers of nepotism and favoritism in an organization the individualistic approach of the American culture, a focus on the personal attributes and skills, as opposed to relationship induced responsibilities is a cultural divide in the managerial process.

Decision Making

Example 5.3

The *ringi* or stamp system is practiced in Japanese organizations to arrive at decisions. Ideas originate in the bottom sections of the company that are closer to the issues engaged and then are passed upward with each higher level adding their approval or stamp signature until

(Continued)

(*Continued*)

it reaches the last stage. At each managerial level a vetting process assures that the final decision is representative of the collective appraisal of all those involved in carrying out the direction or changes that will take place, thereby retaining harmony and common purpose throughout the group.

In some collective societies commercial decision making is more diffused throughout the enterprise with lower and middle level managers participating in the process. It allows for more "let's get everyone on board" by having them participate while also providing for a comprehensive review in which all levels work in tandem for the betterment of the group.

Some individualistic cultures exemplify a marked tendency to centralize decision making retaining all important organizational decisions from strategy to tactical maneuvers to implementation in the purview of a few select indiviudals. Orders originate in the highest echelons of the institution and top down orders are followed along the chain of command, much like a military unit. A more entrepreneurial key man style is employed, as organizational members are predisposed to rely on the firm's founder or successor to guide the company. This dichotomy is not an absolute, as both collective and individualistic cultures do not always follow this example. Collective societies due to high power distance and high-risk avoidance promoting strict organizational hierarchies do place decision making at the top. Individualistic societies due to low power distance and low risk avoidance promote more democratic dispersal of decision making to allow for participation by members of commercial organizations.

Other Aspects of Individualism Versus Collectivism in Commercial Settings

Safety vs. Risk

The old adage *safety in numbers* is reflective of collective societies that see an advantage in existing group oriented agreement on what is expected. Taking chances outside of the norm is viewed as dangerous as the proverb, the *nail that sticks out of the board gets pounded the hardest* is practiced.

Rules and regulations are more strictly followed, as people are more comfortable in knowing what is required from them as determined by group acceptance standards. The uncertainty of the unknown displaces individual initiative with the fear of being ostracized from the group, held up as acting different, and hence losing the protective group veil acts as a safety barrier they will not cross. Individualistic cultures are more risk adverse. They exhibit a willingness to take chances to show that they possess the personal ability to stand out from the crowd and be noticed. They see rules and regulations as more guidelines than absolutes challenging the status quo and perhaps the traditionally accepted norms that the group has imposed. They see themselves not as renegades setting out to destroy but as pioneers to move things forward.

Reward and Penalty Systems

In individualistic societies personnel that do an outstanding job are singled out for their achievements. They are given distinctive material recognition rewards such as raises, bonuses, and promotions. On the other hand when things go wrong specific individuals are singled out for the error, held up for group identification, and passed over for advancement, demoted, or even fired.

In cultures that prize collective effort one is expected to contribute to their team with any form of resulting reward being bestowed equally on the entire group. When things go awry blame is assessed as failure of the group to look out for individual team members and the person responsible feels social shame and embarrassment as opposed to individual disappointment to fulfill their own personal goals. It is the integrated system that is at fault not the individual in it. In such societies one associates their own success with those around them and when they look into the mirror of recognition they do not see themselves but instead a montage of faces looking back.

Procedural Systems

Collective organizations apply rigid formalized procedures to accomplish the goals of the institution enabling those within the system to operate more efficiently and effectively under the assumption that group values and goals will thereby be maintained if all follow the announced system measures. Such reverence is closely aligned with risk adverse cultures as depicted above and reflective of a collective mind-set.

Other associations are more informal with looser paths punctuated by individual involvement thereby allowing for divergent methods of accomplishment to be achieved. Getting things done outside the system, a more risk tolerant environment exists, is acceptable.

Cooperative Efforts

Cooperation to preserve harmony within the group is a basic characteristic of collective societies. Working together with unity of purpose and sharing in accomplishments is valued. In more individualistic societies competition is encouraged as it is thought to bring out the best in people and thereby contribute to the overall good of all concerned. While team projects are utilized in individualistic cultures they are not permanent and usually built on the premises that bringing together the singular skill sets in specialized fields or professions yields, a cross-optimization of ideas, produces the best result.

Stability as Opposed to Innovation and Change

Collective cultures tend to preserve traditions and promote the status quo choosing stability over change. Historic customs, a proven accessorial template, are maintained to guide current and future activities. (A Confucian principle as earlier noted.) People are adverse to risk venturing when the old ways are challenged. Life should follow preordained patterns and may be determined by spiritual influence or karma that cannot be challenged. What was good enough for those who came before us is good enough for us today, a preservation of group endowed policies. All should proceed at a steady rhythmic pace and be at harmony with each other and nature.

Innovational advancement is a hallmark of individualistic societies and the individual can influence the future. Change is viewed as a key element to survival and the pursuit of change is necessary. To be personally dynamic and thereby forge transformation is a valued pursuit as it makes for a better life.

Meeting Characteristics

In individualistic denoted societies, meetings are approached with a pronounced agenda driven consideration. What is to be discussed takes precedence over who will be there and who is presenting ideas. Everyone is presumed to voice their independent critical thinking with the focus on the points being addressed, as they will be valued for their personal idealistic opinions. The quasi informality of the process allows one to challenge another. When the meeting is over there is a presumptive assumption that all is concluded as everyone has had their say.

Collective cultures place much importance on the relationship of people at meetings which themselves are more formal with built-in group protocols. Who are they, what is their position relative to mine tends to dictate responses. They will avoid addressing specific individuals ever cognizant of being respectful and to not upset the harmony of the group in session. How and when points are addressed, whom to challenge and whom to not, are influenced by mutually shared relationship etiquette or codes of behavior that all subliminally recognize. Disagreements are not always voiced but are approached in more informal behind the scene social sessions so that meetings do not always settle matters. I found out in my own career that in eastern societies, over after hour drinks and dinner, that the conversation in the more relaxed atmosphere allowed for issues to be re-approached and for subordinates to express their opinions of the day's events openly. A freer exchange environment prevailed and I learned to hold my own opinions till then. Presented in summary format Tables 5.3 and 5.4 depict the behavioral traits that **tend** to be associated with individualistic and collective cultures.

Table 5.3. Individual Versus Collective Basic Observational Characteristics

Behavioral category	Individualistic cultures	Collective cultures
Chief social interaction unit	Person	Group
Behavior explained by	Personal traits and reactions	Group norms and collective acceptance
Success defined by	Individual ability	Shared attributes and contribution
The self defined by	Individual identity	Group affiliation
Knowledge center	Internal directed, know thyself	External directed, know others
Achievement criteria	Self interest	Group benefit
Goal standard	Personal over group	Place group ahead of individual
Value barometer	Self-assuredness	Modesty
Fear factor	Abhors dependence on others	Fears ostracism by others
Connections to others	Casual and dismissive	Strong and required
Obligations to others	Few and dispersed	Many and interwoven
Confrontation	Acceptable and justifiable	Limited to preserve harmony
Task versus relationship	Task oriented/doing	Relationship oriented/being
Physical space	Personal privacy	Communal openness
Education value	Maximize individual attainment	Contribute to social advancement
Family ties	Relatively unimportant	Primary importance
Society view	Instrument for own personal satisfaction	Duty owed to society in which they participate
Needs	Self-sufficient	Cross-dependency
Time orientation	Short-term	Long-term

Table 5.4. Individual Versus Collective Actions in Commercial Settings

Business arena	Individual culture	Collective culture
Meetings/contact negotiations/agenda	Risk-taking, bold initiative	Patience, caution, incremental improvement
	Spontaneity	Adherence to form
	Outspoken	Periods of silence
	Logical reasoning	Emotional sensitivity
	Clarity, frankness, confronting threatening at times	Indirectness, assuaging, avoidance, save face
	Decisiveness, individual principles	Consensus building, group convention
	Inject legal safeguards, contracts relied on to cover all issues	Build trusted relationships to supplement contractual obligations
	Protect the individual	Maintain group harmony
	Reliance on data	Reliance on precedent, intuition
	Sequential subject matters	Synchronic subject matters
	Transactional focused	Trust and relationship focused
Employees	Proving oneself	Humble cooperation
	Reward performance, track record	Reward seniority, loyalty
	Opportunity oriented	Obligation and dutiful oriented
	Specialists	Generalists
	Autonomous	Dependent
	Low power distance	High power distance
	Competitive	Submissive
	Employment terminable	Employment for lifetime
	Hire best qualified	Relationships impact hiring
	Relationship defined by law	Family obligations and responsibility
	Materialistic, money oriented	Altruistic, social acceptance

The choice of individualism versus collectivism (I-C), further defined as to whether self-construct should follow a socially independent course or alternatively pursue an interdependent track, as a prime controlling cultural value determinant is sustained in a recent article composed by over 30 research contributors from all over the world. In their unified opinion, their "study endorses the unidimensional conceptualization of I-C, because a considerable number of studies on cross-cultural topics in the workplace have adopted such a conceptualization, and found support for its relevance to various employee and organizational outcomes."[14] Their survey of 6,509 managers from 24 countries used the chief criteria I-C as the moderator of work demands. They found that it strongly influenced employees' cognitive, emotional, and attitudinal reactions in the work environment while affecting functional performance and relationship construction at all managerial levels as well as across and between transnational organizations.

SECTION 3
Putting It All Together

CHAPTER 6

Cultural Navigation Techniques

It is not the strongest of the species that survives,
Nor the most intelligent that survives.
It is the one that is the most adaptable to change.
Evolutionary theory, Charles Darwin

An old Yiddish proverb instructs one to remember that "you can't control the wind, but you can adjust your sails." As one ventures into alien territories they will encounter new and different cultural winds. Such changes are a natural phenomenon and global travelers need to carefully stir themselves as they can easily be blown off course. Even the best maps do not necessarily provide the most suitable route. One must therefore be ready to adjust their sails to catch the variances in the prevailing winds. The process is called navigation, adaptation to new surroundings.

Prenavigational Principles

Before embarking on the navigation of cross-cultural waters a few basic principles or predispositions need to be considered.

Cultural Reflection and Refraction

When one views another culture they are in essence looking through a window from their home outwardly into a foreign environment. Images that are witnessed through and even upon the culturally infused glass medium contain elements of refraction and reflection (see Figure 6.1). Reflection occurs when lights bounces off the glass surface, causing a mirror-like effect. This phenomenon allows one to see

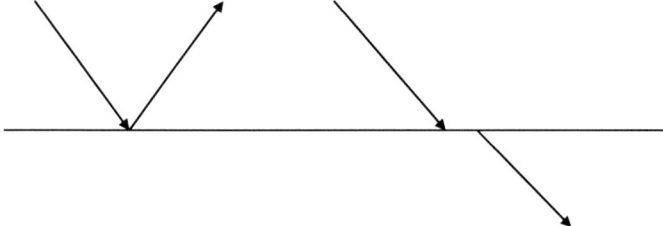

Figure 6.1. Reflection and refraction.

their self-image in the cross-cultural process. By viewing the values of others do we reflect on our own beliefs. This is not specifically culture shock but the bounce back can be unsettling. The reflection may cause one to question themselves, their time honored internal concepts as culture is transgenerational and perhaps undergoes a transformational adjustment to one's own mind-set. Such self-examination, reflection, is normal and an essential part of the cross-cultural learning process. One should not be afraid to examine their own cultural imperatives as encounters with alien cultures put a strain on what we think and what we know. International executives might consider a proverb to help in this adjustment process. "A man's feet should be planted in his country, but his eyes should survey the world," George Santayana, American philosopher.

The process of refraction, where light changes direction, but without reflecting from the surface, depends on how even the surface is. With a smooth surface, cultures similar to those at home, the image is clean and clear. If the surface is rough, the light scatters, starts traveling abruptly in very different directions and the image is bent. This physics phenomenon well illustrates the problem faced by those encountering a culture that is so rough—vastly different or alien from theirs. The unexpected causes a diffused and distorted impression to appear so what one sees is not a clear unencumbered image but is filtered by prejudicial inferences. If one does not take the time to appreciate much less understand the why of dissimilarity the false impressions witnessed can never be adjusted to, and cross-cultural conflicts will always remain. Quick impressions need to be avoided as one's mind requires time to process, understand, and appreciate refracted observations.

The Judgmental Mantra

As one encounters alien social environments they would be well advised to consider repeating the following mantra:

It's not right
It's not wrong
It's just different

Accepting differences and refraining from egocentrically inspired judgmental conclusions will well serve the cross-cultural explorer. It is normal to view variances in black and white absolutes as opposed to relative grains of gray or shading. When one encounters a totally different way of thinking, the assault to the mind causes one to erect barriers of defiance and react negatively. Keeping an open mind is difficult but essential to the cultural education process.

Process of Cross-Cultural Engagement—The OODA Loop

Colonel John Boyd devised an information strategy for warfare that emphasized changing the enemy's behavior as opposed to annihilating their forces. The OODA loop originally designed for the U.S. Air Force in its operational implementations stands for "observe, orient, decide, act."[1] It is a most appropriate template to guide one in conducting themselves in a cross-cultural environment as it forces one not to make assumptions nor rely on stereotypes and avoid egocentrically based judgments. Second, it implores one to familiarize and adjust, to acquaint oneself with the new surroundings and reflect on one's own cultural mind-set before moving on. Third, armed with the two prior considerations, to decide on how best to engage those in a new culturally alien society that best fits the existing circumstances. And last, act having initially appraised the issues involved. A fifth provision could be added—to analyze the results of such actions, constant feedback, and learn from the results produced by such decisions.

The OODA model of engagement is a four stage revolving process built around the central idea of observation and the revolving loop of

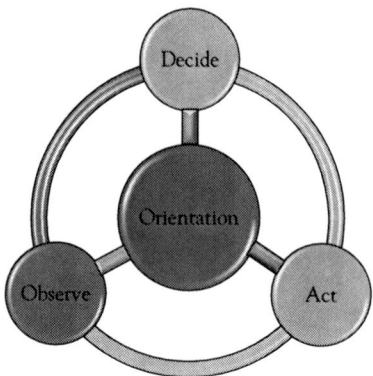

Figure 6.2. OODA *strategic cultural engagement model.*

orientation, decision, and action interfaced with constant feedback (see Figure 6.2). This strategic application well suits cross-cultural engagements as the parallel impetus to not impose one's culture on others, destroying their culturally anchored heritage, but instead looking for (1) key culturally induced motivational drivers and working with them to achieve managerial goals and/or (2) finding common ground to alter or change their behavior to arrive at a mutually satisfactory result. In essence, one attempts to psychologically get inside the mind-set of an alien society and identify their inherent traits that control their inspirations, values, and hence motivational decision making dimensions to establish a base upon which to build symbiotic relationship between dissimilar parties. This approach forces one to be a cultural detective. First, gather facts through observation rather then predisposition, then orient oneself by categorizing what one has observed into usable elements to allow for decision making and finally proceed to action. With continuing feedback to one's actions the process is a revolving one that allows one to continue to adapt.

Observation

It all begins with observation, and it is a constant activity, scanning the new environment and gathering information about it. In essence, acting like a cultural inspector, gathering raw information to better understand how others make decisions that their actions are based upon. As cultures are not stagnant but are in a continuing state of evolvement due to cross-cultural borrowing and diffusion the observation stage is never ending. By first observing, preconceived impressions, prejudicial potentially false impressions of expected behavior can be challenged and eliminated from the cross-cultural equation.

Orientation

The processing of this data, the contextual orientation stage, allows one to build a mental image of the circumstances that trigger a culturally induced response. Synthesizing the collected information can be assisted by cataloging the information into concisely applied sets of value determinants (see Level 1 in chapter 5) and a singular controlling determinant (see Level 2 in chapter 5) in order to rationalize how one approaches their thinking process. One familiarizes themselves by placing labels of understanding, the practical use of cross-cultural determinants upon observed behaviors, instead of starting out with them.

Decision

Armed with the orientated synthesis of the observed raw material characteristics one can better move toward informed decision making and select a course of action. Clarifying the dominant side of the key cultural determinant controlling or influencing the reaction of the other party allows the informed to make the proper decision. It can also be used to uncover the minor hidden conjoined or opposite cultural characteristic and use that as a wedge to alter or change the chief controlling cultural stimulator—creating a bridge of similarly shared values.

Action

As one carries out the conceived decisional approach, the action stage, the results should continuously be observed and one starts the process over. It is a never ending loop with continuing feedback that allows one to move through the four steps faster and more efficiently. Each time the strategy beginning again with the observation stage, the input is narrowed and one moves directly home in the actions required.

Illustrative Case—The OODA Loop in Action

Example 6.1

The Mexican manufactory subsidiary of an American company that supplies the company's worldwide distribution network needs to increase production capacity to meet extraordinary periodic high levels of consumer demand around the world just at month's end. The recently posted U.S. trained plant manager, relying on his experiences running factories back home, is considering requiring an additional employee shift to work on Saturday. As an inducement for the extra time he plans to offer this selected group twice their normal hourly pay time to open the plant on the weekend. His own culturally induced assessment leads him to believe that individuals in that special group will value the extra pay incentive and be encouraged to work the additional day. He announces this consideration and just a few employees sign up.

However, if he first took the time to observe and acquaint himself with his Mexican personnel and learn how they spend their weekends and nonwork periods he would learn that such episodes of time off are devoted to spending time with family and friends. Social activities in the collective Mexican culture are highly valued and take precedence over material rewards—one cannot buy time with loved ones. At the gates of the facility employees arrive in groups, spend their lunch time and other breaks during the day massed together, and leave in unison greeting and chatting with the next arriving group. Their discussions center on relationship building with stories of relatives and friends dominating the conversations. They attend parties and social events together and all are treated like extended family. They see themselves as part of a commonly shared equal social group and when one member or a specified group of individuals is singled out for special treatment the rest react negatively and may ostracize such people as not participating for the widespread good. If he took the time to orient himself with examples of the indigenous culture around him he would have found himself in a better strategic position to accomplish his primary goal. He would have been more culturally focused realizing he is dealing with strong harmonistic group conventions, trusted intergroup relationships, and a traditional desire to maintain group identities. Coupling the observed characteristics he could have matched them with a cultural determinant which best defines and explains what he has observed—individualism versus collectivism. (In fact on the Hofstede scale Mexico ranks low—30 on the individualistic degree meter, per Table 4.1)

But still the local manager needs to get the plant up and running on Saturday. His best decision-making approach is to open the plant for all shifts on that extra day negating the stigma of specialized treatment for one group over the other. He should announce that they all need to pull together and contribute an additional shift for the benefit of all that rely on the company to support them. **But on Sunday**, the customary day for friends and relatives to gather together he should reward all families with a company wide sponsored carnival, entertainment, and picnic to celebrate their generous overtime assistance. He should make a speech thanking not only the employees but appreciative and respectful of their families for their support, stressing that they are the heart and soul of the operations and by coming together at a mutual time of need they participated in the common good. The execution of the action is as important as the action itself with the rhetoric announcing it as well as that used in its wake contributing to its accepted implementation. The ability to speak the language of one's environment with its culturally induced overtones is a must. Connecting with the local culture, both understanding and appreciating where they are coming from is critical to effective management. The manager should closely monitor the party, circulating with his administrative staff to gauge feedback on the taken action, learning how to improve relationships with his employees for the future. The OODA strategic result beginning with the observations of this collectively influenced culture can also be appreciated by the individual oriented manager as he himself takes the time to reflect on his own appreciation of family and friends recognizing the duality of the individual versus collective determinant—it cuts both ways.

The Process of Cultural Drafting

The technique of drafting, also referred to as slipstreaming is technically an engineering process employed to reduce the effect of drag, increasing forward progress by exploiting another's forward or leading position. When two or more objects align in a close grouping the physical matter behind the front item utilizes the slipstream created by it to propel the following object forward. The secondary objective of drafting is pace lining the average energy expenditure reduced thereby conserving power but retaining the same velocity or forward momentum. It also has a similar but slightly smaller effect on the lead object so both objects benefit from the phenomenon. In essence, both the lead and rear objects require less power to maintain their speed than if it were moving independently—a symbiotic mutual value relationship is thereby created.

The physics principle is well known for its use in race car driving but it has a similar application in other competitive forms of racing from bicycle, speed skating, even cross-country skiing and long distance running. For the average automobile driver traveling on a fast highway and slipping in behind a large semitruck to maintain speed with less pressure on the gas pedal is not an urban legend but a realistic result as opposed to moving independently. While staying behind a large vehicle cuts down on the air pressure one encounters in front the drafting or slipstreaming effect is also in play. Also referred to as cooperative fluid dynamics, the system is found in nature as well. Flocks of birds, especially during the migration season, are seen overhead flying in a V formation. The wingtip or aerodynamic pattern enables the front bird to engineer an up-wash circulation of air so that those behind it receive a lift force and do not have to work as hard to achieve optimum distance with less exerted internally generated power. Some scientists have hypothesized that lobsters moving through the ocean as opposed to air use a single file formation called trains to achieve a similar result and perhaps fish swimming in schools are also practicing this principle of group positioning induced forward momentum. Others discount these ideas in nature and just think it is merely a follow the leader physical manifestation at work as it is hard to exactly measure the efficiency achieved by these species in formation.

The term slipstream in colloquial English also refers to a method whereby the act of following closely behind another person produces a beneficial result for the trailing party. Letting another take the lead takes the pressure off the secondary person as they rely on the one in front of them to provide direction, choose the best route, and avoid hazards. Simply put, they do not have to work so hard to achieve a competitive result and can coast on the tails of those in front—much like a flock's V formation.

Strategic Business Drafting

While not precisely referred to as drafting commercial entities have used this principle in their strategic plans and tactical maneuvers. As firms began to move overseas they quickly learned that the cultural headwinds they faced in alien territories were best navigated by forming associations with other parties more knowledgeable about local foreign market conditions. That the time and energy needed to understand these new areas of exploration could be discounted by appointing overseas distributors to handle sales in them. Expanding on this principle the use of foreign licensees or forming joint ventures also began to be used. Even if companies wished to have a strong controlling capital interest it was more prudent to use a brownfield entry model, buy a local existing organization, as opposed to a greenfield initiative and creating anew. These are all forms of strategic cultural drafting although financial investment motivations and other considerations are also at play in the decision. The idea of cultural drafting is in essence cooperative competitive recognition or learn from the other guy and these entry strategies recognize such a key deliberation—cultural differences.

Organizational Cultural Drafting

The same principle as used in mechanized movement in auto racing, and perhaps nature, is applied in cross-cultural dynamics. As firms venture into alien cultures the staffing of the managerial cadre for foreign assignment consists of three pools of potentially hirable talent. They are:

1. Domestic country nationals
2. Host country nationals
3. Third country nationals

The first category, domestic country nationals (DCNs), are citizens of the company's home or headquarters nation. When placed abroad they are known as expatriates, those being located away from their native country and place in another. While they are familiar with the organization's domestic culture, their placement in alien societies, even with cross-cultural training is still a daunting task to master. DCNs are best utilized when cross-cultural skills are not paramount to the job task at hand and a smooth efficient liaison with the home office is the driving motivator. When the assignment does not bring such placed individuals into daily contact with local society, DCNs are best suited for foreign assignment. Technical or mechanical oriented short-term required expertise correlates well with DCNs as opposed to long-term sales and marketing positions as well as embedded human resource administrators.

The second group, host country nationals (HCNs), are citizens and/or long-term residents of the specific nation the firm wishes to operate in. They are deeply familiar with the culture of the host market and come with a built-in sensitivity and an understanding and appreciation of local customs, traditions, and practices. But on the other hand, they have a reverse cultural issue, dealing effectively with the company's headquarters staff. They find themselves explaining to those in the originating domestic market why their particular country requires varied approaches and different alterations with regard to expectations as well as strategies and tactical methods to achieve them. HCNs are best utilized in societies that are vastly different from the home country headquarter culture where they can act as on-site interpreters of local conditions that are deeply unfamiliar. As previously noted HCNs are best suited to work alongside native networks such as indigenous manufacturers and suppliers as well as locally maintained retail channels of distribution and the aligned fields of marketing where advertising and promotional efforts need to be highly customized to suit the local business environment.

The last option, third country nationals (TCNs), are neither citizens of the firm's headquarters country nor of the local nation they are assigned. Hence they maybe be referred to as duel expatriates as they are not native to the country they are assigned to nor the home country of the company hiring them. They tend to be culturally neutral, comfortable to a degree with the society of the entered market while cognizant of the home territory culture. They are valued for their ability to effectively straddle the two diverse cultures acting as a mutually respected middleman. TCNs are best utilized in situations when trust issues between countries are a prime consideration.

Outside these employed personnel, managers who know they will be engaging a cultural group different then their own often hire temporary or specific project linked professionals to assist in navigating the cultural matrix. Such people act as facilitators or guides. They may be as simple as a translator to provide a cross-communication service or the more sophisticated host country legal firm. Intermediary consultants with a specific knowledge of and perhaps contacts in a certain local industry or governmental agencies can also be hired. While these parties have a valued host country cultural indoctrination they are not always familiar with the culture of dual foreign parties engaging their services.

In the end, all of these aforementioned players need some degree of training to be effective in their diverse citizenship roles but by using them to draft behind, those less familiar with cross-cultural conditions can move faster with less knowledge in alien environments.

Managerial Cultural Determinant Drafting

Beyond employment specialists or short-term outside professional agents global managers are often pressed to take a direct and more personal role as they engage, work with, and form relationships with foreign parties. Many cultures recognize that in order to gain their trust they want to foster a principal to principal interaction and association.

It is at this level that the concept and use of cultural drafting using one's knowledge of each party's dominant determinants can play a large part in successfully navigating the complex cross-cultural world. As noted in chapter 2 one's cultural indoctrination is a stumbling block, our ingrained Achilles heel as culture hides more than we realize and what it hides best is our own cultural prejudices. It is our blind side and the sophisticated international executive recognizes this fact. It is natural to first assume that the world is like us and hence our actions are prompted by an ingrained pattern of behavior that is hard to disobey. We take the lead in pushing our own procedural agenda and expect the other party to respond in a similar fashion. Or the other party recognizing our cultural disposition uses it to maneuver us toward a resolution they favor. A few examples from my own international business career show how the cultural drafting technique by others or myself was successfully utilized.

Time Orientation Drafting

Example 6.2

My most vivid example of the use of differences in time orientation occurred with my Japanese contacts. On trips to Japan my American compatriots and I would advise our hosts with precise timetables for our visits. Our air arrivals and departures were requested and they were nice enough to arrange for all transportation arrangements for which we were most grateful. When the Japanese team visited us we acted in kind but were kindly told that they had a series of other meetings scheduled and hence they would make their way to our offices on their own. They never told us when they would arrive, only the first day they wished to meet with us, nor did they advise when they would be flying home stating they would be staying as long as needed. We dismissed their desire to never reveal their exact travel plans without much thought. But there was a methodology to their intent. They knew in advance our preoccupation with schedules. Knowing the day we arrived and the day we planned to leave gave them an advantage. They used our time sensitivity against us. All important concessions they wanted were postponed until the last day and hour of our meetings as they knew we would be reluctant to alter our plans and dare not head home without accomplishing something. In the interim, they entertained us lavishly with numerous social functions. As time began to dwindle on the day of our departure they assured us they would arrange to get us to the airport on time. They were not in a hurry but they knew we were. On the other hand their visits with us at headquarters were slow and deliberate. Not knowing when they planned to leave worked in their favor. A number of times they would ask to be excused and could we reschedule another meeting a day or two later. Sometimes they told us that they had other business in the country and would be back to finish our business in a week's time.

The Japanese simply drafted onto our time orientations letting our desired expectations work against us. [Reader Ref: Time orientation: Japan 80/high long-term versus US 29/short-term, per Table 4.1].

Power Distance Drafting

Example 6.3

My business associates in 1970s Panama were a family enterprise well into their fourth generation when I began to use their organization as a distributor handling local government administered duty free at borders and airport shops and non-U.S. military PXs (commissaries) in Latin and South America. Our pricing to this intermediary was very sensitive and an important consideration in successfully marketing in such retail distribution outlets. Not only due to heavy competition in our industry but at that time certain allowances had to be made to those overseeing local entrance into these facilities necessitating that our distributor attain very reasonable margins for their efforts on our behalf in order to handle such additional expenses. My negotiations began with the youngest son of the family who was about my age and primarily responsible for our relationship, but it soon proceeded upward to the eldest and then finally the patriarch of the business who had the final say. At each stage the price demands for lower and lower prices ensued. As the newly appointed American export director for the region I certainly wanted to impress my superiors but I was out in the field alone and felt I carried an impressive decision making title. My Panamanian friends knew this, making sure to laud my insecure abilities and praise my naïve talents. They on the other hand practiced high power distance with a stricter organizational higher hierarchy and would never allow such sensitive negotiations to be handled, much less settled by lower family members. American managers in lower managerial echelon positions tended to over reach their decision making responsibilities due to their lower power distance. They used such knowledge and understanding as a maneuvering tool by allowing me access to their top decision making person, forcing me to be equal to the task. While I should have reserved judgment and advised them I had to first get approval of my bosses at headquarters, my own power distance indoctrination allowed me to finalize all arrangements on the spot. While business proved to be good they drafted onto my own cultural tendencies and I got pulled along in the process of my own slipstream. If I had recognized what they were doing I might have gotten a better deal for my company.[Reader Ref: Power distance: Panama 95/high versus US 40/moderate per Table 4.1].

Uncertainty Avoidance Drafting

Example 6.4

Working for a U.S. company that was the licensee of a high-end French designer house fragrance line we had the right to create American style boxed gift sets to serve the specialized needs of our domestic customers at Christmas time. Boxing fragrance with bath powder, lotions, scented soap, bath beds as well as boudoir and bathroom accessories was an extremely popular item for the holiday season and hence a valuable contributor to our marketing and sale programs. Such packaged presentations were, however, outside the traditional French taste and were not offered in their markets nor the worldwide distribution channels they used, with the exception of the American market. The Australian distributor for the same French house admired the American gift set approach, felt it would be successful in their country and asked to purchase such items from us. The request was granted but under the condition that only the items approved by the French could be sold to them.

The yearly presentation to the Managing Director, whose family founded the renowned French firm, of the American gift set collections was made by me as Export Director of the company. The French deeply guarded their prestigious brand and were staunch traditionalists in regard to the industry they felt they created.[2] They strongly felt that the purity of fragrance should be limited to perfume as presented in singular crystal decanters and/or colognes, a less potent version of the perfume extract, and such versions in decorated glass bottles only. Such elegant presentations were a throw-back to the original sale by the historically prestigious perfume shops of Paris. The sanctity of such a traditional limited packaged appearance had been ingrained in me during my initial visit with French company executives and observed first-hand as I toured the channels of distribution throughout France. A ingrained high risk aversion to changing the old ways permeated their decisional mind-set. Tampering with time-honored packaging presentations was taboo and the French only tolerated the American alterations as long as they were limited to our country, an unsophisticated market with bourgeoisie customers, while offering them a very sizable financial royalty. Instead of trying to convince the MD to embrace a new marketing direction and take a chance, a decidedly American cultural characteristic, I always opened our meetings with a gracious

(Continued)

recital of his thinking to show I shared his high risk avoidance. By embracing and using the French cultural outlook I deflated his normal argumentative position, showed him I respected his reluctance, which I understood and shared. In doing so, I was able to get his agreement to approve some of the new packaging for the Australian Christmas season; additional sales for my export division. I drafted onto his cultural stance allowing me to maneuver him. [Reader Ref: Uncertainty avoidance: US 46/low propensity versus France 86/high propensity per Table 4.1]

Individualism Versus Collectivism

Example 6.5

An American firm I consulted for had a Bolivian tin resource extraction operation and needed to replace its on-site retiring general manager. Two candidates emerged. One was the son of a wealthy local investor, part of the historic Spanish landed gentry, who initially attended boarding school in Massachusetts and was further educated at Texas A&M majoring in mining along with an MBA from Arizona State University in global supply chain management. He never worked in a mine but for two years was part of the U.S. company's headquarters staff in Houston, Texas and tagged as a rising executive. The other was an indigenous native of Bolivia who began working in the local mine when he was 12, delivering food and water to the underground workers. Now 45, he had handled every job in the facility and worked his way up to shift supervisor becoming an admired local hero in the mining community, extolled for his personal success. In the end, management chose the local Indian native feeling that his extensive knowledge and experience coupled with the respect he enjoyed amongst the other miners were paramount considerations. After just 3 months the mining operations were falling way below historic production results. Disputes amongst the workers resulted in periodic work stoppages, equipment malfunctions were on the rise and safety issues plagued the site. Despite the constant meetings with his staff the new manager wasn't making any progress. Feeling frustrated, being accused of "selling out" to foreign corporate management and for the first time

(Continued)

(*Continued*)

alienated by his own people the new manager quit. The other candidate was hastily flown in to replace the disgraced general manager and over the next 3 months activities returned to their normal levels and in fact even began to garner improvement.

The U.S. company, having similar operations around the world, decided to hold a postmortem meeting on what went wrong in the hopes of gaining some insight to direct them for the future as general manager vacancies materialize in other foreign ventures. The discussion centered on the initial judgment of the human resources department explaining that in Bolivia, culturally a collective society, it was felt that a local native trusted and accepted by his peers seemed to be the natural choice. What did they miss? I explained to them what while Bolivia is a collective society, as are most South American societies, top leadership assumption does not naturally arise from those within the group as existing fostered relationships get in the way. For a member to assume a hierarchical position, especially an authoritative commanding role, those in the group assume an individualistic acceptance posturing. While it was OK for the native Indian to have a supervisory "blue collar" level role in the mine itself working next to the other miners like himself in their mutual daily tasks, the elevation to a "white collar" supreme authoritative position in an independent office with control duties and responsibilities beyond their shared historic group goals disrupted the unity and harmony he once shared with them. Their culturally driven collective dimension was fractured and the relationship with his comrades changed. He could no longer address them on an equal level as he was no longer part of them. However the placement of the communal outsider as the general manager, whose birth pedigree and education set him apart from the regular workers was simply more acceptable to them. Even though they operated within an overwhelmingly distinctive collective dimension the workers could draw on the hidden or dormant part of their own cultural personalities and recognize individuality. Instead of trying to become one of them, a normal narrative when placed in a collective society, individualism worked to his advantage. In essence, the local Bolivian workers wanted to draft onto American cultural thinking and be pulled along. This allowed them to rationalize the decision as outside of their control.

CHAPTER 7

Final Thoughts

Culture is engaged over a wide open range
and one needs to have a wide vision as
the horizons are always changing

The book opened with a profile of East versus West, a symbolic reference to the cultural divide that global managers face as they embrace the tide of globalization that has and will always influence their international venturing. The commercialization of the world, international trade is the prime motivator for engaging other cultures, and as such is a natural platform upon which bridges of common understanding and appreciation of differences can be constructed. Samuel P. Huntington's well worn phrase "clash of civilizations"[1] is not a comment so much on the ideological dissimilarities between people but an observation of how varying societies conduct their material life choices, exhibited by the values attached to the exchange process. Hence many cultural misunderstandings are rooted in the mercantile process, the trade initiative, as outside war the cross-territorial trade process is what brought people into the most contact with alien societies. In the modern era of globalization this consideration is even more acute. Upon the review of all collections of value dimensions as well as sets of collateral cultural influential determinants a common denominator has emerged, the base upon which the universally applied paradigm of inspection and examination is constructed. It is mankind's relationship to others, the group around them, in other words the interplay between the individual and one's entourage, one's collective disposition. This singular dimension, the nucleus upon which a template for research is devised and cultural determinants emanate from is individualism versus collectivism.

If managers can construct a *via media* (middle path) that straddles this dual cultural dimension in their relationships and associations around the world then they will be well on their way to mastering the complex matrix of cross-cultural differences. From the old testament, The Book of Ezekiel, chapter 37, verses 16 and 17 often interpreted as prophesizing the eventual coming of one secular blessed state, such as Israel, or alternatively a unified religious organizational institution for the world, is told as an inspirational message from the Lord God with instructions to:

> "..take a stick of wood and write on it Judah. Take another piece of wood and write on it Joseph. Bring them together… and they shall become one in your hand."

Such hallowed verse signifying opposite sides that are unified into one applied instrument is also recited in the new testament, the book of Mormon and even alluded to in the Koran as the patriarch of all Western religious beliefs under umbrella direction of Abraham and his proposition of a monolithic supreme deity. This directional principle, to recognize the conjoined duality in life, is also represented in the Eastern philosophy of a Yin and Yang and symbolized by the Roman heathen in religious terminology and their demigod Janus; is the right method to employ cultural determinants. Always recognize the duality inherent in all cultural differences and aim to construct cross-cultural relationships on the similar elements contained in each determinant as opposed to concentrating on the opposites.

Collateral Elements Toward Cross-Cultural Understanding

Being culturally proficient is not just a function of knowing, understanding, and applying one primary or a group of the most influential cultural determinants to a new alien society. While such a managerial tool to assist in the engagement of and the forming of workable associations with alien societies is a valuable guiding instrument it should be tempered by observation before application. Relying on just a limited set of cultural determinants or perhaps one key dimension is like the proverbial saying that if all you have is a hammer every project looks like a nail.

While such guidance is helpful it is akin to learning the mechanics of a foreign language without taking the time to gain the wisdom to appreciate the context in which communication flows and the relationship of the parties to the conversation—knowing why and how to use words and phrases. A greater sophistication resulting in more well rounded cultural introduction is required. One must take the time to learn the history, politics, and economics of foreign countries that give rise to its traditions, customs, and belief systems and form the platform upon which culture is constructed and used.

Rule-Based Versus Relationship-Based Cultures

Outside the cultural differences that separate societies affecting managerial activities, Shaomin Li in a 10-year project to understand what he calls the "Asian miracle" of economic performance[2] concludes that East Asian countries are relationship-based whereas the Western societies, America and Western Europe, are rule-based. In defining these societal characteristics, the Asian Way and Western Way, he makes a veiled reference to cultural determinants by explaining that the deeply rooted Confucian values in the East emphasize long-term outlooks and reciprocity in interpersonal relationships. In essence, he is referring to time orientation, the future, and pronounced collectivism; both of which are part of the five-point Hofstede determinant collection and form two of my own four-point first-level filtered determinants.

His extensive examination of the relationship factor describes the Chinese *guanxi* culture, a version of which is also practiced in other East Asian countries. Social networks are at the core of the concept stating "Everyone must have his or her circle of close friends" with the members of numerous circles helping "each other in social interactions and exchanges," creating a system of mutual monitored assistance.[3] This is clearly a description of a collective society. Li directly references another Hofstede determinant stating "there is a greater (high) power distance in relationship-based organizations" while mentioning that communication in such societies is "high-context," a Hall defined dimension.[4] A closer look at Li's well researched and presented evidentiary descriptions of these two governance systems, relationship- and rule-based, indicates they are driven by cultural influences even though his labels do not use such descriptive language.

While Professor Li and this author share the same publisher and collection editors I find myself not dismissing so easily the influence of culture on these alternate social environments impacting the management of commercial affairs. Li opens his first chapter with the story of a group of Chinese having dinner together after a day of intensive meetings noting that it is a typical scene he has experienced with Chinese business people. When the waitress inquirers toward the end of the meal if they want to pay together or separate checks? "Together!" someone in the group shouts, and then a heated discussion breaks out over who should pay. He remarks that "if you think that we were trying to get someone else to pay, then you are wrong. Each of us competed for the bill."[5] Using this illustration Li asks why do some groups, like the Chinese always compete to pay while others, mostly Americans, "go Dutch" when a group of people eat out? I do not feel the answer is based on periodic swings in socially induced governance systems but simply on traditional conditioning traceable to a cultural determinant called individualism versus collectivism.

Global Ethical Approaches Influenced by Culture

As stated in my book, "Ethics is a branch of moral philosophy. It is a set of principles to govern human conduct as practiced by a particular person as well as in concert with a specific society or culture group."[6] All behavior has an ethical component. Ethical decision making, the guide of behavioral responses, is contextual, taking place within the confines of distinctive social environments. For the individual, it is deeply influenced by or conceivably controlled by the dominant cultural values affecting morality that one grows up with and is exposed to over time. Such ethical perceptions can be challenged; however, when one encounters an alien culture whose moral principles conflict with prior programming. The idea of an ethical dilemma, often encountered by the embedded managers of multinational corporations in foreign countries, occurs when one is confronted with alien ethically defined values that conflict with the prevailing and accepted ethical principles uniformly practiced in the manager's home country. The rightness or wrongness of managerial actions can therefore be subject to alternative judgmental determinations that are dependent on cross-cultural practices. The duality factor found in cross-cultural dimensions also affects cross-cultural ethical choices. In theoretical terminology a split in applying ethical determinations divides ethical imperialism and cultural relativism. Ethical imperialism directs one as they encounter alien societies to continue to apply those principles garnered from their home or domestic society, ingrained culturally driven determinations, to consider them universally appropriate and treat them as core human values applicable anywhere, any time, under any condition and for any relationships, an internal individualistic approach asking one to rely on their own ethical judgmental initiatives. The polar counter balancing weight to ethical imperialism is cultural relativism. This directive instructs one that "no culture's ethics are better than any other's; therefore there are no international rights and wrongs. Respect for the ways and behaviors of others, their culture, traditions and customs, is the paramount guideline."[7] In simplified terms *When in Rome, do as the Romans do*, an external collective imperative forcing one to appreciate varying group induced ethical judgments.

The concept of duality, the symbiotic relationship of two elements contained within each other as first introduced in chapter 4 can be illustrated in its ethical context by the following picture (Figure 7.1). Initially the dominant portion is visible as when one first views the above words they first see **GOOD** as displayed in black letters. But upon close inspection of the white portion, outlined by black letters, the world **EVIL** emerges. Readers please excuse the reference to good and evil in the world to again exemplify the duality paradigm, although the visualized thought is the basis for a good deal of world literature and to many it represents the Taoist philosophical concept of Yin-Yang, two balancing forces, the duality of morality.

Figure 7.1 The duality of ethical conduct.

Cross-Cultural Training

Studying Culture—The Push Back Factor

Those studying or taking any type of course training in cross-cultural issues may feel negative connotations about the subject matter. The reaction of those being introduced to cross-cultural issues can range from apathetic to threatened to outright hostile. Some participants in educational programs are (1) merely ambivalent and view the subject matter as irrelevant while others (2) expressing an ethnocentric attitude, as noted in chapter 1, consider their culture superior so, "why learn about inferior ones, all should think like me." Still others (3) are fearful that exposure to different beliefs and ideas, be they secular or religious, may weaken or threaten theirs. They see it as a patriotic duty owed to their political or spiritual affiliation to not entertain or reject outright alien cultural nationalism in any form of others. Whatever the reason for the reluctance to embrace a cross-cultural indoctrination, the emotional feeling is real and is the first obstacle that must be addressed. This matter needs to be confronted in a more direct manner as it has a tendency to be pushed aside or indirectly handled with kid gloves, as opposed to an outright head-on tackling of the issue. If the stage isn't set to allow for a free and open presentation of culture any instruction offered will either fall on deaf ears or will be dismissed as irrelevant.

First, to combat what some consider a personal assault on their heritage it is worthwhile to first explain that the study of culture is a two-way street, and not a one-way trip, that the starting point is oneself. One must know where they begin before setting out on a journey from their culturally induced home port. They will not be asked to abandon their cultural anchor but take it with them to be used in whatever alien waters they travel. To understand and appreciate differences one must first examine themselves. If anything, the study of others helps to strengthen one's convictions, not lose them. It is the lack of familiarity that breeds contempt, fosters distrust, and destroys relationships creating a false wall of misunderstanding.

Second, that the study of culture does not emphasize differences but is used to find similarities that assist in building a bridge of commonality upon which relationships can be constructed. The duality factor inherent in all cultural value determinants, as previously presented in chapter 4, indicates that while a dominant characteristic may primarily drive a person's decisions, behavioral responses, and perceptions, our opposite hidden, masked, or dormant subservient still exists and it can be used to match up to another's prevailing traits.

Third, diversity is not a bad thing. Tackling the problems of life is a shared endeavor by all people and one can learn how to best handle their own issues if they have a 360° view of how others accomplish their goals and tasks.

In the end given, and as recounted in chapter 2, our growing commercially globalized world, a cross-cultural education is an essential tool for mangers to practice the art of getting things, which is their prime purpose.

The object of cross-cultural training is fourfold. First, to combat apathy or noninterest, threatening, or outright rejection as noted above. Second, to counter stereotyping and preconceived notions about others for a more neutral field upon which the engagement of alien cultures is allowed to flourish. Third, to combat culture shock that is damaging to one's emotional well being if one fails to overcome the fear of ambiguity, uncertainty, and differences. And last, to arouse sensitivity and empathy when one encounters a culturally alien environment, and foster tolerance.

Final Thoughts

Authors look to close their work with choice words that both exemplify the underlying theme of the book while concluding with inspiring rhetoric that resonates with the reader. Let me borrow a line from another writer to do so. Ron Suskind in his latest political nonfiction account of the latest Presidency offers a profile of Obama as he embraces his new position plagued by trying economic times. He describes his ascension to the role stating that "In the yin of crisis he seemed to spot the yang of opportunity."[8] Using the Chinese philosophical reference, and perhaps playing off the previously noted make-up of the Chinese word for crisis, danger, and opportunity, he weaves a nice reference. A similar metaphorical approach also works for cultural guidance. Recognizing the duality factor, that in all things the opposite exists, one should be prompted to follow an analogous cross-cultural guiding reference "In the yin of difference one should search for the yang of similarity." Instead of focusing on what separates us as human beings we should strive to uncover what we have in common and use it to construct bridges across the global cultural chasm. Such pedagogy directs one to follow Occam's Razor directive and aim for the simplest, most direct route as business managers, and perhaps all of us as we engage alien societies. This directive prods one to respect diversity but embrace similarity and perhaps use a singular tool, individualism versus collectivism, to construct bridges of connection across differences.

As one studies cross-cultural matters it is wise to heed an old academic axiom that the function of education is to expand the mind, not fill it with facts. Hence, first study those you come into contact with and then categorize such observations into sets of cultural determinants, interpretation guidelines, that help you understand them. Remember that one has to deal with people the way they are, not how you would like them to be. Finally, while the prime motivation in the study of cross-cultural issues is to learn how to better work with alien societies in furtherance of mutually beneficial goals, an often overlooked benefit is that the process also allows one to learn about themselves. Through the mechanisms of getting to know how others think and react the opportunity to reflect and conduct a self-examination of one's own values emerges. Appreciating oneself, what makes us tick, and understanding how our own mind-set controls our own individual behaviors and reactions to the world around us increases our interpersonal skills. A cross-cultural indoctrination cuts two ways as it strengthens us both internally and externally.

Globalization drivers along with technology as discussed in chapter 2 have pushed more companies to value an overseas presence. This increased commercial interaction and communication, more and more people working together, tends to construct bridges across the cultural divide by encouraging the convergence of cultural systems.[9] This development of the worldwide value chain "implies a trend toward lower CD (cultural distance) over time albeit at different paces across the globe."[10] This phenomenon has also increased the continuing process of acculturation, defined as the changes induced in systems as a result of the diffusion of cultural elements in both directions,[11] also provides for the reduction in CD between two or more societies. These two integrated events, one pushing the other, have reduced differentiation and promoted similarities. Historic geographical proximity between nations coupled with modern economic unions have allowed inherently different cultural groups to lower their respective CD as both factors encourage cross-cultural distribution.

Simply put, the process of globalization, be it commercially generated or just a product of greater social integration via acculturation and geographical nearness, is in itself a generator of cultural sharing that in the end results in greater similarities being felt. With due reverence to Dr. Shankar and others that have used the term CD in their research writings perhaps this often used term is a negative misleading past identification idiom, as it places focus on what separates us as opposed to what brings us together. Maybe it needs to be replaced by a better, more positive phrase like CS, cultural similarity, placing emphasis on what we all share. This change in terminology would push people to look for commonalities in human values as the prime precipitator of our behavior towards others as opposed to a differentiation quotient. Managers studying culture might then be predisposed to approach the subject matter in a more affirmative framework.

On the subject of CD (cultural distance), some scholars argue that most distance constraints oversimplify the relationship between countries, that they overlook subjective and context-specific nature, ignoring the mechanisms through which distance operates. They feel that "Essentially, international management is management of distance," in essence organizing "cultural, administrative and economic" factors that separate societies.[12] While it is hard not to agree that different sovereign nations have alternating political and socioeconomic systems they overlook the fact that we now live in a *borderless world* with *interlinked economies*,[13] where the structures upon which global business are conducted are getting more uniform than ever before. Technology links the commercial world together like never before and global competition is forcing the same opportunities and problems on all parties; the world is flatter.[14] However, putting aside disagreements on political or economic systems being different or becoming more similar, culture is about people. At the core, humans want the same things out of life, they just go about achieving them in numerous ways, the different mechanisms they employ. If one can learn to focus on the commonalities we all share then we can construct bridges across to link up with the cultural similarities in our lives and not differences. Approaching culture is akin to the proverbial seeing a glass as half empty or half full. Half empty is a negative connotation with focus on the need to fill the disparities between societies, the empty space deemed as cultural differences. Half full is a positive consideration because it recognizes that there already exists progress in the cross-cultural process and all one needs to do is build on what already exists. I see the cultural glass as half full.

Striking a Balance in the Diversity Issue

Firms of the future, compelled to embrace the world community for their output and input— the global sales and supply chain system—are also encountering a new diversified labor force and associated affiliations. This simple fact is changing the game as companies are compelled not only to recognize cultural diversity but hopefully to see the value of it. Globalization without localization strips away diversity encouraging mono-cultures to supersede multicultures in society and organizations. Through our desire to organize, manage, scale-up, coordinate, and control we have tended toward encouraging mono-cultures where we seek to normalize behavior, and in turn reduce organizational (and wider socioeconomic) resilience. It is diversity that unleashes creativity; it is diversity that helps create conditions conducive to change. It is this important dynamic, globalization but recognizing localization, which is fundamental to ensuring vital resilience for organizations in the future.

Therefore, managers must be global in outlook while local in behavior. The global imperative needs to be constructed on shared values while the local initiative respects the multicultural aspect of the world. Managers should strive to build on what we all culturally have in common but remain equally cognizant that differences still exist and if balanced correctly successful cross-cultural engagements will result. They need to champion unified goals in their organizations and with outside affiliates while realizing that the mechanisms to reach them are varied. In the end however all are headed in the same direction and this is the unifying magic of culture.

If you go out into the world armed only with your own culturally induced observations and sentiments, you will surely find yourself on very weak ground. You will lack an understanding of the arguments, convictions, and the coherent views of other realities and perceptions that you'll need when challenged by differences. An old Talmudic saying tells us that "we don't see things as they are, we see things as we are." One's cultural indoctrinated mind-set clouds the interpretation of life around us. It acts like an automatic unrecognized filter of our sensatory inputs causing us to prejudicially judge the behaviors of others. It is truly our Achilles heel.

Good international managers envision alternate realities. One may find that the things their own society values are not the things that are valued by others. The sets of organizing principles one has become accustomed to are usually not universal.

Being a part of a tradition doesn't mean suppressing your individuality. Applying the culturally based traditions of others to a new situation is a creative, stimulating, and empowering act. All things require tradition, as without it everything is impermanent and in constant flux but it doesn't mean one needs to be stuck in theirs.

Most professors would like their managerial students to be more rebellious and argumentative. But rebellion without a rigorous alternative vision is just a feeble emotional spasm. Being open and aware of different surroundings and varying mind-sets allows for the alternative to be considered. If I could offer advice to a young global manager it would be to rummage through one's own culture for a body of thought that helps you understand and address the differences you will see around you. Give yourself a universal label. If your education hasn't provided you with a good knowledge of countercultural viewpoints then it has failed you and you should try to remedy that ignorance by retaining an open mind that recognizes dualities of thought as we all harbor them. The proverbial direction that instructs one to *think outside of the box* contains a cross-cultural imperative.

To include the ideas and approaches that one normally applies to a situation is enlarged and improved by allowing oneself to view issues from the prospective and mind-set of different cultures. In fact, a cross-cultural education allows one to not just think outside the box but *turn it upside down, empty it, and start by filling it anew.*

One must also be aware that cultural differences using the multiple dimensional criteria of the most quoted researchers have a tendency to be viewed and hence applied as polar opposites with the implication that on a 360 scale a 180° of difference separates cultures. This misconception tends to result in an unintended construction of falsely presented tectonic splits in cross-cultural appreciation. The result is that such indoctrination causes us to approach the subject like a true–false exam question as opposed to a multiple choice format. There are relative degrees of difference and in fact most cultures are separated by a variance of 30°. We are simply much closer to each other, more the same than different. If the accent is placed on what we share as opposed to what separates us the cultural gap will shrink and bridges of commonality can be more easily built.

Metaphorical Conclusions
The U.S. Cultural Misinterpretation

The American society has been poetically portrayed as a "melting pot," the assimilation of indigenous and immigrant cultures to form a unified nation. While such lyrical depiction is intended to invoke a common bond of the country's people there is a better imagery to define the United States. The nation is more like a *salad bowl* in which a variety of individual vegetables all with their unique tastes, textures and colors are covered by a uniform salad dressing, the bonding agent. Such description best fits the country as it recognizes our individualistic and grouped nature, the Yin and Yang of a any society. Such terminology well illustrates how the core element of culture, not just that of the United States but all nations of the world, individualism and collectivism are mutually shared properties symbiotically combining to strengthen and hold the world together. We are all more the same then different processing elements of both cultural determinants.

A good lesson to be learned from not trying to force everyone into a uniform society is well stated in the commonly heard expression, "no one size fits all." Diversity is part of the natural order of things and cross cultural multiplicity serves to strengthen not weaken us.

The Cultural Crayon Box

Children all over the world over use crayons at home and in school while restaurants often distribute them to adolescent guests to keep them occupied. A box of crayons offers an array of color choices with some weird identification names given some of them. Some have sharp points while other after use are dull. Some deliver a brilliant shade while others are lackluster. Absent the chemical pigment that gives them a distinctive tint or shade they all have as their base element a waxy substance called paraffin. But in the end they are all called upon to function together contributing, with their individual uniqueness, to collectively produce a color picture. Just using one color would not deliver the complexities nor the intricate details that truly represents the needs and desires of the artist. Young children everywhere recognize the value of applying differences to one of their first creative endeavors, scribbling on a sheet of paper with a writing instrument, a crayon. Inherently they apply diversity in the form of using varying colors to express themselves and accomplish their earliest adolescent tasks.

A crayon box is a good metaphor for the combined use of varying human societies around the world and their special cultural characteristics. International managers should be encouraged to utilize the varied global culture box to help achieve a successful result to their strategic intensions for their companies.

The metaphor of a child's crayon box revisits the book's Introduction illustrations of early adolescent behavior. Such examples were presented in the hope that when we operate in grown up adult environments we should consider reverting back to our childhood and approach cross cultural differences with the acceptable naiveté and initial ingrained tolerance of our youth before such valuable traits were learned out of us. An open mind allows for the seeds of a cross cultural indoctrination to germinate and grow thereby bettering the person and improving the relationships they wish to create with others. A closed mind reduces our capacity to expand ourselves while limiting the successful engagement of others around us. Global managers must possess an open mind.

Notes

Preface

1. Nohria (2011), pp. 14–15.
2. Cabrera (2012).
3. Velo (2012), Preface.
4. Moua (2010).
5. Holiday (2012), p. E12.
6. Harris (1983), p. xviii.

Introduction

1. Song lyrics by Oscar Hammerstein II with music by Richard Rodgers (1949). A 1958 movie version and a 1961 TV program were made from the original play with a revival on Broadway in 2008. In the musical the song is used to explain racial prejudice.
2. Author note: This phrase was the title of an article by Thomas L. Friedman writing in the business section of The New York Times on August 14, 2011, p. 11, offering an explanation of the current common denominator merging young people and the middle class into a worldwide explosion of frustration rallying against economic problems. The phrase has probably been used by other writers to express similar considerations.
3. Kipling (1892).
4. Author note: *Buttons and Bows* is a song published in 1947. The music was written by Jay Livingston with lyrics by Ray Evans. New York, Sony/ATV Music Publishing. The most popular version of the song was recorded by Dinah Shore in 1947 and reached the charts the following year.
5. Campbell (1972, pp. 61–62).
6. Diamond (1999).
7. Finely (1973).
8. Koehm (2011).
9. Morris (2010).
10. Ferguson (2011).
11. Morris (2010), p. 144.
12. Ferguson (2011), p. 15.
13. Ferguson (2011), p. 17.
14. Ferguson (2011), p. 97.

15. Author note: *Come Together* is a song published in 1969 by The Beatles. It was written primarily by John Lennon but credited to John Lennon and Paul McCartney. The song is the opening track on The Beatles' album Abbey Road, New York, NY, Big Seven Music Corp.

Chapter 1

1. Ferraro (2006), p. 19.
2. Tylor (1871), p. 1.
3. Herskovits (1955), p. 305.
4. Hofstede (1991).
5. Hall (1976).
6. Ferraro (2006), p. 19.
7. Hofstede (1999).
8. Deal (1982).
9. Johnson (1988), pp. 75–91.
10. Cox (1997).
11. Harris (1996), p. 140.
12. Song title and lyric, *Bridge over troubled water* published in 1970 with words and music by Paul Simon, New York, NY, Columbia Records.
13. Ferraro (2006), p. 35.
14. The term has been attributed to those describing the uncanny ability of Apple Computer founder Steve Jobs to motivate others by misleading his audience into believing that the task at hand could be accomplished, in spite of the realities of difficulty surrounding a project. The phrase may have been borrowed from the popular *Star Trek* science fiction TV program and movie series to explain a phenomenon whereby normal observations are altered causing the brain to not to perceive things as they really are.
15. Bellah (2011).
16. Kissinger (2011).
17. Aydon (2007), p. 1.
18. Angier (2011); referencing David Wilson.
19. Delanty (2011).

Chapter 2

1. Bergreen (2007), p. 235.
2. Ferraro (2006), p. 31.
3. Yule (1998).
4. Bergreen (2007), Author note: numerous translations and editorial editions of the original book have been published and they are listed in the Bergreen

book beginning with Polo, Marco, (1955), La Description du Monde, edited by Louis Hambis, Paris, France, Librarie C. Klincksieck.

5. Petrekis (2011).
6. Scheidel (2010), p. 18. Author note: In an editorial note the author of this commentary notes that the Aristotelian style work under the Latin title *Oeconomica* was not written by Aristotle but does not ascribe another author to the work.
7. Figueria (2009), p. 9.
8. Crespo (2008).
9. Scheidel (2010), p. 145.
10. Scheidel (2010), p. 114.
11. Boesche (2005).
12. Shamisastry (1915).
13. Rothbard (1990).
14. Chow (2007), p. 13.
15. Ghazanfar (2000), p. 857, citing Ihya 1 : 17.
16. Scheidel (2010), p. 87.
17. Koehn (2011).
18. Cohen (2011).
19. Sullivan (2011).
20. Raushenbush (2011).
21. Ferrero (2006), p. 19.
22. Friedman (2011), p. 312.
23. Friedman (2011), p. 71.
24. Shankar (2012).
25. Hofstede (1994).
26. Friedman (2008), Hot, Flat and Crowded, (2005), The World is Flat, (1999), The Lexus and the Olive Tree.

Chapter 3

1. Copeland (1985).
2. Morrison (1994).
3. Hodge (2000).
4. Harris (1996).
5. Harris (1996), p. 53.
6. Derensky (2010).
7. Edfelt (2010).
8. Adler (2008).
9. Mor Barak (2011).
10. Konopaske (2004).

11. Early (2003).
12. Kluckholm (1961), p. 11.
13. Condon (1975).
14. Hofstede (1980).
15. Ronen (1985).
16. Brake (1995).
17. Trompenarrs (1998).
18. Author note: Based on the original research of Parson (1951).
19. Hall (1996).
20. Everett (2012). Author's note: Readers are also directed to Everett's first book, *Don't sleep, there are snakes* (2008), an account of his life amongst the Piraha an isolated Amazon hunter-gather tribe whose customs and language remains remotely alien with stark contrasts to those of any other society on earth.
21. Author's note: The original source of this often used proverb is a bit hard to track down. John Bartlett's, "Familiar Quotations," attributes its genesis based on the research of Christopher Martin Wieland to the author Musarion in his work Canto II (1768) writing in German, "Die Herren dieser Art blendt oft zu vieles Licht; Sie sehn den Wald vor lauter Baumen nicht" which has been translated to "Too much light often blinds gentlemen of this sort. They cannot see the forest for the trees." See: Bartlett's Familiar Quotations: A Collection of Passages, Phrases, and Proverbs Traced to Their Sources in Ancient and Modern Literature, 17th Ed. (2002) by John Bartlett and Justin Kaplan. New York, NY, Little, Brown and Co.

Chapter 4

1. Beer (2003), p. 255.
2. Li (2011), p. 17.
3. Scheidel (2010), p. 13.

Chapter 5

1. House (2004), p. 12.
2. House (2004), p. 12.
3. Gladwell (2008), pp. 202–207, 220.
4. Gladwell (2008), p. 232.
5. Gladwell (2008), p. 214; quoting Ho-min Sohn, a Korean linguist.
6. Campell (1972), p. 61.
7. Campell (1972), p. 61.
8. Fukuyama (2011).

9. Trivers (2011).
10. Haidt (2011).
11. Author note: Those readers interested in appreciating the onerous labor intensiveness of rice production and the requisite need for the expertise of the individual farmer are directed to consult the concise description offered in chapter 8 "Rice Paddies and Math Tests" contained in Outliers by Malcolm Gladwell, 2008, London, UK. Allen Lane—Penguin Group, pp. 224–227.
12. Gladwell (2008), p. 238.
13. Author note: reference to the TV show of the same name—*Have Gun—Will Travel* staring Richard Boone, was a popular American Western television series that aired on CBS from 1957 through 1963.
14. Yang (2012).

Chapter 6

1. Friedman (2011), p. 9.
2. Author note: Statement not entirely true as the anointment of the body with scents was used thousands of years ago and practiced by many different civilizations around the world.

Chapter 7

1. Huntington (1998).
2. Li (2010), p. *Author's Notes* at the beginning of the book.
3. Li (2010), p. 25.
4. Li (2010), p. 92.
5. Li (2010), p. 1.
6. Beer (2010), p. 1.
7. Beer (2010), pp. 147–148.
8. Suskind (2011), p. 34.
9. Webber (1969).
10. Shankar (2012), p. 6.
11. Berry (1980).
12. Zaheer (2012), p. 19.
13. Ohamae (1990).
14. Author note: see series of books by Thomas L. Freidman (1999), (2005), and (2008).

Bibliography
of Recommended Cases
on Cross-Cultural Studies

The Lincoln Electric Company: Venturing Abroad, Harvard Business School, no. 376–029, 1976.

Philips versus Matsushita: A New Century, A New Round, Harvard Business School, no. 5-302-063, 2001.

Wil-Mor Technologies: Is There a Crisis?, Richard Ivey School of Business, no. 9A99M042, 2003.

Intel In China, Richard Ivey School of Business, no. 9A99C007, 1999.

Hans Fritz at Novartis Thailand (A): The First Month, Harvard Business School, no. 9-399-123, 1999.

Ellen Moore(A): Living and Working in Korea, Richard Ivey School of Business, no. 9A97G029, 2000.

Black & Decker-Eastern Hemisphere And The ADP Initiative (A), Richard Ivey School of Business, no. 9A98G005, 2004.

The Global Leadership of Carlos Ghosn At Nissan, Thunderbird, The Gavin School of International Management, no. A07-03-0014, 2003.

Textron Ltd., Richard Ivey School of Business, no. 9B01M070, 2002.

References

Adler, N. (2008). *International dimensions of organizational behavior* (5th ed.). Mason, OH, Thompson.

Angier, N. (2011). *Thirst for fairness may have helped us survive.* New York Times, Retrieved July 5, 2011, from: http://www.nytimes.com/2011/07/05/science/05angier.html?nl=todaysheadlines&emc=tha2

Aydon, C. (2007). *The story of man, an introduction to 150,000 years of human history.* New York, NY: Carroll & Graff.

Beer, L. (2003). The gas petal and the brake...Toward a global balance of diverging cultural determinants in managerial mind sets. *Thunderbird International Business Review 45*(3), 255–273.

Beer, L. (2010). *A strategic and tactical approach to global business ethics.* New York, NY: Business Expert Press.

Bellah, R. (2011). *Religion in human evolution.* Cambridge, MA: Belknap Press/Harvard University.

Bergreen, L. (2007). *Marco Polo, from Venice to Xanadu.* New York, Knof.

Berry, J. (1980). Social and cultural change. In H.C. Triandis & R.W. Brislin (Eds), *Handbook of cross-cultural psychology, Vol 5* (211–279), Boston, MA: Allyn & Bacon.

Boesche, (2003). Kautilya's arthasastra on war and diplomacy in ancient India. *The Journal of Military History 67*, 9–37.

Brake, T., Walker, D. & Walker, T. (1995). *Doing business internationally; The guide to cross cultural success.* New York, NY: Irwin.

Cabrera, A. & Unruh, G. (2012), *Being global: how to think, act and lead in a transformed world,* Cambridge, MA: Harvard Business Review Press.

Campell, J. (1972). *Myths to live by.* New York, NY: Penguin.

Chow, G. (2007). *China's economic transformation* (2nd ed.). Malden, MA: Blackwell, p. 13.

Cohen, R. (2011, November 8), Don't disregard importance of defining culture, Phoenix, AZ, Arizona Republic, p. B9—first published in the Washington Post.

Condon, J. & Yousef, F. (1975). *Introduction to intercultural communication.* Indianapolis, IN: Bobbs-Merrill.

Copeland, L. & Griggs, L. (1985). *Going international, how to make friends and deal effectively in the global marketplace.* New York, NY: Plume.

Cox, T. & Beale, R. (1997). *Developing competency to manage diversity: Readings, cases and activities.* San Francisco, CA: Berrett-Koehler.

Crespo, R. (2008). *On Aristotle and Economics*. IAE Business School—Austral University, DT 11, retrieved June26, 2011 from http://www.iae.edu.ar/piDocumentos%20Investigacin/Working%20Papers/DTIAE08_2008.pdf

Deal, T. & Kennedy, A. (1982). *Corporate cultures: The rites and rituals of corporate life*. New York, NY: Harmondsworth–Penguin.

Delanty, G. (2011). Cultural diversity, democracy and the prospects of cosmopolitanism: a theory of cultural encounters. *The British Journal of Sociology 62*(4), 633–656.

Derensky, H. (2010). *International management: Managing across borders and culture* (7th ed.). Upper Saddle River, NJ: Pearson Prentice-Hall.

Diamond, J. (1999). *Guns, germs and steel*. New York, NY: W.W. Norton.

Early, C. & Ang, S. (2003). *Cultural interactions: Individual actions across cultures*. Stanford, CA: Stanford University Press.

Edfelt, R. (2010). *Global comparative management, a functional approach*. Los Angels, CA: Sage.

Everett, D. (2012). *Language: The culture tool*. New York, NY: Pantheon.

Ferguson, N. (2011). *Civilization, the west and the rest*. New York, NY: Penguin.

Ferraro, G. (2006). *The cultural dimension of international business* (5th ed.). Upper Saddle River, NJ: Pearson Prentice-Hall.

Finely, M. I. (1973). *The ancient economy*. Berkley, CA., University of California Press—note 2nd ed. 1985 and updated 1999.

Freidman, T. (1999). *The lexus and the olive tree*. New York, NY: Farrar, Straus and Giroux.

Friedman, T. (2005). *The world is flat*. New York, NY: Farrar, Straus and Giroux.

Friedman, T. (2008). *Hot, flat and crowded*. New York, NY: Farrar, Straus and Giroux.

Friedman, T. & Mandelbaum, M. (2011). *That used to be us*. New York, NY: Farrar, Straus and Giroux.

Fukuyana, F. (2011). *The origins of political order*. New York, NY: Farrar, Straus and Giroux.

Ghazanfar (2000). The economic thoughts of Abu Hamid Al-Ghazal and Thomas Aquinas: Some connective parallels and links. *History of Political Economy 31*(4), p. 857 citing Ihya 1:17.

Gladwell, A., (2008). *Outliers, the story of success*. New York, NY: Allen Lane, pp. 202–207, 220.

Haidt, J. (2011). *The righteous mind*, New York, NY, Pantheon.

Hall, E. T. (1976). *Beyond culture*. Garden City, NY: Doubleday.

Harris, W. (1983) *The womb of space*, Westport, CT, Greenwood.

Harris, P., & Moran, R. (1996). *Managing cultural differences* (4th ed.). Houston, TX: Gulf.

Herskovits, M. J.(1955). *Cultural anthropology*. New York, NY: Knopf.

Hodge, S. (2000). *Global smarts*. New York, NY: John Wiley & Sons.

Hofstede, G. (1980). *Cultures consequences : International differences in work-related values*. Beverly Hills, CA: Sage.

Hofstede, G. (1994). *Cultures and organizations.* New York, NY: Harper Collins.

Hofstede, G. (1991/1997). *Cultures and organizations: Software of the mind.* New York, NY: McGraw-Hill.

Hofstede, G (1999). Problems remain, but theories will change: The universal and the specific in 21st-century global management. *Organizational Dynamics* 28(1), 34–44.

Holiday Mathis/Creators' Syndicate (2012, March 22nd), *Horoscope*, Phoenix, AZ, The Arizona Republic.

Huntington, S, (1998). The clash of civilizations and remaking of world order (1st ed.). New York, NY: Simon & Schuster.

Johnson, G. (1988). Rethinking incrementalism. *Strategic Management Journal* 9, 75–91.

Kipling, R. (1892). *Barrack-room Ballads* 75, London, England, Methuen & Co.

Kissinger, H. (2011). *On China.* New York, NY: Penguin.

Koehm, N. (2011, July 3). *The moral behind all the numbers.* New York, NY: The New York Times, p. BU 7, referencing Sedblacek, T., (2011) Economics of Good and Evil), Oxford Press, Oxford, England.

Koehn, N. (2011, October 23). *The tale of the dueling economists.* New York, NY: New York Times, BU, p. 8 referencing Wapshott, N. (2011), *Keynes-Hayek: the clash that defined modern economics*, New York, NY, W.W. Norton.

Konopaske, R., & Ivancevich, J. (2004). *Global management and organizational behavior.* New York, NY: McGraw Hill–Irwin.

Kluckhohn, F., & Strodbeck, F. (1961). *Variation in value orientations.* New York, NY: Harper & Row, p. 11.

Li, S. (2010). *Managing international business in relation-based versus rule-based countries*, New York, NY: Business Expert Press.

Mor Barak, M. (2011). *Managing diversity, toward a globally inclusive workforce* (2nd ed.). Los Angels, CA: Sage.

Morris, I. (2010). *Why the west rules—For now.* New York, NY: Farrar, Straus and Giroux.

Morrison, T., & Conoway, W. (1994). *Kiss, bow or shake hands*, (1st ed.). New York, NY: Adams Media.

Moua, M. (2010). *Culturally intelligent leadership—Leading through intercultural interactions.* New York, NY: Business Export Press.

Nohria, N. (2011 – July 24). *Looking ahead behind the ivy.* New York Times, Education Life, pp. 14–15.

Ohamae, K. (1990). *The borderless world.* New York, NY: Harper Business.

Parson, T. (1951). *The social system.* New York, NY: Free Press.

Petrekis, (2011), Cultural background and economic developmental indicators: European south vs. European north. *Modern Economy* 2(3), 324–334.

Raushenbush, P. (2011). *Religion, morality and the financial industry: an interview with chief rabbi lord sacks.* Retrieved October 25, 2011 from: http://www.huffingtonpost.com/paul-rauschenbush/chief-rabbi-lord-sacks-interview-religo

Ronen, S., & Shenkar, O. (1985). Clustering countries on attitudinal dimensions: A review and synthesis. *Academy of Management Journal*, September, 449.

Rothbard, M. (1990). Concepts of the role of intellectuals in social change towards laissez-faire. *The Journal of Libertarian Studies* 9(2), Fall.

Shamisastry {Arthashastra} translations, (1915). Retrieved March 15, 2007 from: http://.msu.edu/projectsouthasia.history/primarydocs/Arthashastra/index.htm

Shenkar, O. (2012). Cultural distance revisited: Towards a more rigorous conceptualization and measurement of cultural differences. *Journal of International Business Studies* 43(1), 1–11.

Sheidel, W. & Von Reden, S. (2010). *The ancient economy*. New York, NY, Routledge, p. 2, 13 referencing: Finley, M. (1973). *The ancient economy*. Berkley, CA: University of California Press.

Simon, P. (1970). *Song title and lyric, "Bridge over troubled water."* New York, NY: Columbia Records.

Sullivan, A. (2011). *The Vatican's radical ideas on financial reform*. Retrieved October 25, 2001 from: http://swampland.time.com/2011/10/24/the-vatican-radical-ideas-on-financial-reform/

Suskind, R. (2011). *Confidence men*. New York, NY: HarperCollins.

Trivers, R. (2011). *The folly of fools, the logic of deceit and self-deception in human life*. New York, NY: Basic Books.

Trompenaars, F. & Hampton-Turner, C. (1998). *Riding the waves of culture* (2nd ed.). New York, NY: McGraw-Hill.

Tylor, E. (1871). *Origins of culture*. New York, NY: Harper and Rowe.

Velo, V. (2012). *Cross-cultural management*. New York, NY: Business Expert Press, referencing Hofstede, G. at: http://www.geert.hofstede.com

Webber, R. (1969). Convergence or divergence? *Columbia Journal of World Business* 4(3), 75–83.

Yang, L., Spector, P., Sanchez, J., Allen, T., Poelmans, S., Cooper, C., Lapierre, K., O'Driscoll, P., Abarca, N., Alexandrova, M., Antoniou, A., Beham, B., Brough, P., Carikci, I., Ferreiro, P., Fraile, G., Geirts, S., Kinnunen, U., Lu, C., Lu, L., Moreno-Velazquez, I., Pagon, M., Pitariu, H., Salamatove, V., Siu, O., Shima, S., Schulmeyer, M., Tillemann, K., Widerszal-Bazyl, M., Woo, J. (2012). Individualism-collectivism as a moderator of the work demands-strain relationship: A cross-level and cross-national examination. *Journal of International Business Studies* 43(4), 424–443.

Yule, H. & Cordier, H. (1998). *Cathy and the world thither*. New Delhi, India, Munshiram Manoharial.

Zaheer, S., Schomaker., M., Nachum, L. (2012). Distance without direction: Restoring credibility to a much-loved construct. *Journal of International Business Studies* 43(1), 18–27.

Index

Announcing the Business Expert Press Digital Library

Concise E-books Business Students Need for Classroom and Research

This book can also be purchased in an e-book collection by your library as

- a one-time purchase,
- that is owned forever,
- allows for simultaneous readers,
- has no restrictions on printing, and
- can be downloaded as PDFs from within the library community.

Our digital library collections are a great solution to beat the rising cost of textbooks. e-books can be loaded into their course management systems or onto student's e-book readers.

The **Business Expert Press** digital libraries are very affordable, with no obligation to buy in future years. For more information, please visit **www.businessexpertpress.com/librarians**. To set up a trial in the United States, please contact **Adam Chesler** at *adam.chesler@businessexpertpress. com* for all other regions, contact **Nicole Lee** at *nicole.lee@igroupnet.com.*

OTHER TITLES IN OUR INTERNATIONAL BUSINESS COLLECTION

Collection Editors: **Tamer Cavusgil, Michael R. Czinkota, and Gary Knight**

- *Assessing and Mitigating Business Risks in India* by Balbir Bhasin
- *Conducting Market Research for International Business* by S. Tamer Cavusgil
- *Born Global Firms: A New International Enterprise* by S. Tamer Cavusgil
- *Emerging Trends, Threats and Opportunities in International Marketing: What Executives Need to Know* by Michael R. Czinkota
- *Managing International Business in Relation-Based versus Rule-Based Countries* by Shaomin Li
- *A Strategic and Tactical Approach to Global Business Ethics* by Lawrence A. Beer
- *Understanding Japanese Management Practices* by Parissa Haghirian
- *Doing Business in the ASEAN Countries* by Balbir Bhasin
- *Tracing the Roots of Globalization and Business Principles* by Lawrence A. Beer
- *Successful Cross-Cultural Management A Guide for International Managers* by Parissa Haghirian
- *Practical Solutions to Global Business Negotiations* by Claude Cellich
- *Trade Promotion Strategies Best Practices* by Claude Cellich
- *China: Doing Business in the Middle Kingdom* by Stuart Strother

CPSIA information can be obtained at www.ICGtesting.com
Printed in the USA
BVOW020124010612

291451BV00005B/5/P